Barbie™

A VISUAL GUIDE TO THE ULTIMATE
FASHION DOLL

Dorling **DK** Kindersley

LONDON, NEW YORK, SYDNEY, DELHI, PARIS,
MUNICH and JOHANNESBURG

Senior Art Editor Lisa Lanzarini
Senior Editor Marie Greenwood
Designer Laia Roses
Consultant Editor Jacqueline Jackson
Managing Art Editor Jacquie Gulliver
Senior Managing Editor Karen Dolan
DTP Designers Jill Bunyan and Andrew O'Brien
Production Jo Rooke and Nicola Torode
Consultants Carol Spencer and Robert Opie
Text by Marie Greenwood, Jacqueline Jackson,
Robert Opie, and Carol Spencer

Photography
Scenes (pages 50–51; 56–57; 58–59; 64–65; 68–69; 60–71; 74–75; 80–81) by Geoff Dann;
vintage dolls photographed by Geoff Dann and by Gary Ombler at the DK Studio.
Mattel photography by Scott Fujikawa, Susan Kurtz, Dave Bateman, Steve Alfano,
Judy Tsuno, and the Mattel Photo Studio

Acknowledgments
Background artworks by Sarah McMenemy.

The publisher would particularly like to thank:
The staff at Mattel, Inc., especially Vicki Jaeger, Lisa Weiner, Lisa Collins, Monica Lopez, Holly A. Stinnett,
Lorraine Alkire, Diane Kapantzos, Suzanne Schlundt, Helene Frost, Michele McShane, Judy Tsuno,
Stella Hopkins, Danny Palumbo, Kitty Black Perkins, Caroline Brockman, Sharon Verduzco, Carol Robinson.

First American Edition, 2000

01 02 03 04 05 10 9 8 7 6 5 4 3 2

Published in the United States by
Dorling Kindersley Publishing, Inc.
95 Madison Avenue
New York, New York 10016

Color reproduction by Media Development, UK
Printed by Artes Graficas Toledo, Spain
D.L. TO: 1885 - 2000

Barbie Ultimate Fashion Queen. -- 1st American ed.
p. cm.
ISBN 0-7894-6664-3
1. Barbie dolls--History. 2. Barbie dolls--Clothing--History. 3. Fashion--United
States--History. I DK Publishing, Inc.
TS2301.T7B25 2000
688.7221--dc21

see our complete
catalog at
www.dk.com

Barbie™

A VISUAL GUIDE TO THE ULTIMATE
FASHION DOLL

DK

A Dorling Kindersley Book

Contents

Foreword by Ruth Handler.............7
Introduction: Doll Story.............8

1 A HISTORY IN PICTURES

A Star is Born.............*12*
Queen of Fashion.............*14*
Sixties Chic.............*16*
Swinging Sixties.............*18*
Flower Power.............*20*
Seventies Style.............*22*
Superstar!.............*24*
International Doll.............*26*
Nineties Barbie.............*28*
Barbie Now!.............*30*

2 HOME IS WHERE THE HEART IS

Home Sweet Home.............*34*
Urban Living.............*36*
Fit for a Princess.............*38*
A Look Inside.............*40*
Kitchen Cool.............*42*
Beauty Time.............*44*
Sweet Secrets.............*46*

3 FASHION AND FANTASY

Springtime Stunners.............50
Spring Picnic.............52
On Vacation.............54
Fun in the Sun.............56
Fall Fashions.............58
Fall Gold.............60
Winter Wardrobe.............62
Winter Wonderland.............64
Disco Girls.............66
Dancing Queen.............68
Out on the Town.............70
City Girl.............72
Bride to Be?.............74
Blushing Bride.............76
What Shall I Wear?.............78
Glamorous Night Out.............80

4 BE ANYTHING!

The Collectibles.............84
Fantasy Dolls.............86
Career Girl.............88
Dolls of the World.............94
Sports Dolls.............100
On the Catwalk.............104
Bob Mackie.............108
Starstruck.............110
Stage and Screen.............112
The Barbie Dynasty.............114
Friends and Family.............116
Changing Face.............120
Packing Up.............122

Reference

Catalog of Dolls
and Outfits.............124
Index.............128
Acknowledgments.............128

FOREWORD

by Ruth Handler

WHEN MY DAUGHTER Barbara was young, she and her friends frequently played with paper dolls. They were adult dolls, and the girls played "growing up" – being a teenager, having a career, being a mother. I saw that this was different than the traditional role play surrounding the baby dolls or companion dolls available for girls, and that there was a definite need for a different kind of doll that would give girls the chance to interpret the adult world in all sorts of ways.

Girls needed to explore the world around them – and Barbie® doll helped show them the endless possibilities available to them. Barbie could be everything they wanted to explore: their everyday lives, careers they could investigate, and the great appeal of the glamorous adult "dress-up" world. Playing with Barbie encouraged little girls to actively use their imagination. Through Barbie they projected themselves into their individual dreams of growing up, and they were able to express their interpretation of the adult world around them.

As the interests of girls changed, as well as the world around them, so did Barbie. Barbie doll reflected the fashions and attitudes of the times, regardless of the era. Always in step with the current styles, her clothes had a quality and detail never seen before in American toy manufacturing. The tiny garments with miniature zippers, snaps, buttons, and buttonholes were yet another way Barbie mirrored a girl's world.

Why has the Barbie doll been so successful for over 40 years? Barbie was designed to fill a girl's need for role playing, so she could work through growing up, exploring her dreams and future. She is the familiar friend of so many girls, and a major part of their lives, helping them dream about the future and its endless possibilities.

Ruth Handler

Introduction

My Lady Betty (1895) came complete with a selection of charming outfits

DOLL STORY

CHILDREN HAVE ALWAYS loved playing with dolls. The ancient Greeks made dolls out of baked clay, and wooden dolls began to appear in 15th century Europe. In Victorian times, dolls were dressed to look like miniature adults, just as children were. But the mass production of dolls really took off in the Fifties, and once Barbie had arrived on the scene in 1959 the doll market was never to be the same again.

Blue lady
This china doll of the 1860s is dressed in the formal fashions of the day. The skirts are drawn back in swags to form a train.

The Victorian Age

During Victorian times, fashionable, finely detailed costumes adorned the more expensive dolls. Papier-maché dolls were molded by machine, while a more realistic face was achieved by shaping wax, bisque, or china, with the body and limbs made from cloth or kid. In the 1860s, dolls began to swivel their heads, but it was not until the 1890s that "sleeping eyes" were invented.

Baby Doll

From the early 1900s, baby dolls became more popular. Doll materials changed, too. Cheaper models began to be made from celluloid, an early form of plastic. The flesh tones were created by adding a pink pigment to the surface, which was then varnished.

Paper dolls
The paper doll was a cheaper alternative to the china doll. Popular from the 1840s, paper dolls were originally hand-colored, and came with a large range of fashionable costumes.

A child points at the doll she wants for Christmas (1937)

Baby face
This sweet baby doll from the 1920s is made from celluloid – a form of plastic that was light, but fragile and flammable.

Girls playing with their favorite dolls (1928)

Blue-eyed baby
This beautiful baby doll was made in Japan for export in the 1930s.

Baby Boomers

In the 1950s, the development of plastics and vinyl made a decisive change to the doll market. These materials were washable and kissable and yet retained their color. Another major advancement came in 1957, when it became possible to root the hair directly onto the doll's head rather than glue a wig onto the surface. Dolls that could walk and talk soon became all the rage.

A little girl cuddles her favorite doll (1954)

Vinyl doll from the 1950s

Both these dolls resemble baby dolls, rather than paper dolls, with their large babyish heads

Miss Revlon dolls by Ideal had both easy-to-style hair and a wardrobe

The Jill doll by Vogue came with a teen wardrobe and featured outfits for sock hops and parties

Pull the ring and hear Cathy chatter!

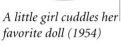

Bild Lilli was made from celluloid

Betty Field (1943)

Betty Grable (1951)

Chatty Cathy

Created by Mattel in the late 1950s, Chatty Cathy soon became a best-seller. Cathy's magic lay in the random phrases she could say when a ring was pulled at the back of her neck. She came with her own clothes that were sold separately.

Dream Teen

As rock 'n' roll grew in popularity, the idea of the "teenager" was born. It was not long before the teenage doll arrived complete with fashionable outfits, jewelry, nylon stockings, and high-heeled shoes. This paved the way for the arrival of the ultimate teen doll: Barbie.

Before Barbie

Fashion model dolls soon became popular – ranging from paper dolls 8 in to 12 in (20 cm to 30 cm) tall with fashion model figures to glamorous play dolls that came with a large wardrobe. Other dolls were sold without additional fashions, such as the Bild Lilli doll. All were predecessors to Barbie, the doll that Mattel founder, Ruth Handler, dreamed of creating as a new American fashion doll with endless additional fashions that were sold separately.

JUDY HOLLI
PAPER DOLLS
Authorized Edition

Paper dolls

Paper dolls with their own fashion wardrobes were great favorites with little girls in the 1940s and 1950s.

Clare McCardell paper doll book 1956

The first Barbie

Mattel's Barbie doll made her debut in 1959 at the New York Toy Fair, priced at a modest $3.00. Buyers were at first skeptical about this 11½ in (29 cm) fashion doll, because it was so unlike the baby dolls of the time, but Barbie was soon to prove them wrong.

WELCOME TO THE WORLD OF BARBIE

SHE IS AN INTERNATIONAL FASHION
DOLL WHO REFLECTS THE HOPES AND
DREAMS OF LITTLE GIRLS EVERYWHERE.
THIS IS HER STORY.

A HISTORY IN PICTURES

1

A STAR IS BORN

FROM THE MOMENT Barbie first appears in 1959, she wins the hearts of people everywhere. Barbie offers something new – a teenage fashion doll with real style. Ever since, Barbie reflects the changing world of women.

SUBURBAN SHOPPER
In the late Fifties women wear hats and sometimes gloves while shopping.

Very slim waist

Ponytail

Barbie doll's first hairstyle is a fashionable ponytail with curly bangs in blonde or brunette.

Later, a red-haired version is introduced named "Titian," a popular term for red hair at this time.

1959

Titian hair

Brunette hair

Ultra long legs

Trimmed with fruit, her shopping bag is the latest California fashion

PICNIC SET
Casual denim jeans are usually worn for outdoor activities like fishing.

Real cork wedgie shoes

THE FIRST BARBIE DOLL
Barbie is a different kind of doll. She has a fashion model's shape and a definite bust. Her coy sideways glance, arched brows, and red lipstick make her look sophisticated. At first Barbie is sold in a bathing suit and the outfits are usually bought separately.

EVENING SPLENDOR
This elegant outfit with matching coat and dress is typical late Fifties formal party wear.

Gloves are essential for formal occasions

1959

This label tells you that each Barbie outfit is the genuine article. A label is attached to the wrist when the doll is first purchased.

RESORT SET
Barbie is ready for a weekend of sailing. Short shorts are very fashionable.

Jumper

FRIDAY NITE DATE
Teenagers wear this style of dress for parties and dates.

Felt appliqué shapes

BUSY GAL
Barbie wears a stylish suit to work as a fashion designer.

1960

Portfolio of sketches

SOLO IN THE SPOTLIGHT
Barbie could be a nightclub singer or a TV show host in this slinky dress.

Balenciaga designed this glamorous gown – dresses like this are popular during this era

This fluffy white stole is detachable

KEN ARRIVES
In 1961 Barbie meets her one and only boyfriend. Ken is good-looking and has his own wardrobe.

Ken doll's special label appears for the first time

REGISTERED NURSE
Barbie cares for the sick in a typical nurse's uniform with its navy blue cape.

Some outfits for Ken are similar to those worn by the movie star Troy Donahue

Movie star Grace Kelly models a wonderful creation in the Fifties

Nursing School Diploma

OPEN ROAD
Barbie is dressed for a drive in her convertible sports car in a car coat coordinated with stylish striped capri pants.

1961

ENCHANTED EVENING
This fabulous satin evening gown is inspired by the glamorous look of movie stars of the day.

1960

Real toggles and embroidered loops

WHAT A CAR!
Barbie takes Ken for a spin in her coral Austin Healey. With its wire wheels, it is the latest thing in sports cars.

1961

Barbie wears the Bubble Cut hairstyle – made immensely popular in the Sixties by First Lady Jacqueline Kennedy

Bubble Cut

1962

BALLERINA
Barbie dances her first solo as the Sugar Plum Fairy in the *Nutcracker Suite* ballet.

Ballet shoes with ribbon ties

Booklets like these come with each doll and separate fashion outfit in the early days. They show other Sixties outfits that are available.

GARDEN PARTY
This cute cotton dress is perfect for a garden tea party. Its wide, flouncy skirt gives the appearance of stiff petticoats, which young women are wearing at this time.

Fully lined in white satin

RED FLARE
This cotton velveteen swing coat is a classic of its time! The cute pillbox hat and long gloves are must-have accessories for the well dressed woman.

Straw hat with salmon red hat band

1962

DREAMBOAT
A sports jacket and slacks are what every well dressed man wears on the weekend.

GRADUATE BARBIE
Barbie graduates from college.

What fashionable women are wearing in the early Sixties

CAREER GIRL
It's 1963, and elegant professional women choose tailored tweed suits with large collars.

Stylish orange-trimmed jacket

TENNIS ANYONE?
Barbie joins the fitness trend and takes up tennis.

QUEEN OF FASHION

THE FASHION OF THE SIXTIES starts quietly with two-piece suits taking center stage. Barbie reflects the interests of an all-American girl – she babysits, goes to the prom, graduates from college, and starts a new career!

1963

Molded hair allows Barbie to wear wigs

1962

Tiny gold-colored buttons

Baby in its own bassinet

Alarm clock

Telephone

Soda and pretzels

WEDDING PICTURE
The wedding dresses that Barbie wears are regularly updated to suit the latest fashions, but she and Ken never actually get married!

SWEATER GIRL
Two-piece cardigan sets were all the rage in the early Sixties.

BABYSITTER
For students like Barbie, babysitting is a great way to earn extra cash.

FASHION QUEEN
This year, wigs are the very latest thing. Barbie has a wardrobe of wigs in three different colors, plus a wig stand.

Barbie's
TEEN-AGE FASHION MODEL
WIG WARDROBE
ON WIG STAND
• BUBBLE-ON-BUBBLE
• SIDE-PART FLIP
• PAGE BOY

BY MATTEL

1963

BLACK MAGIC
For that special evening out, Barbie wears a tulle coat over a fitted black sheath dress.

Satin edging and tie

Black gloves and a gold fabric clutch purse

ALLAN
Midge finds a boyfriend, Allan, who is good friends with Ken.

GENUINE *Allan* T.M.
BY MATTEL

First appearance of a personal label for Allan

1964

GENUINE *Skipper* T.M.
BY MATTEL®

SKIPPER
Barbie is thrilled to have Skipper as a sister. She has her own petite-sized wardrobe.

Skipper has straight red hair. She also comes with blonde or brunette hair

A new, sweptback hairstyle for Barbie, called a "Swirl" ponytail

Swirl ponytail

MISS BARBIE
In her pink yarn cap with gold glitter, Miss Barbie is unique in having eyes that open and shut.

1964

This lipstick is bright red originally

RAINCOAT
Barbie is ready for that rainy day in her sunny yellow trench coat and rubber boots.

Matching umbrella

1964

Barbie goes to the prom with Midge and Ken

Midge comes as a blonde, redhead, or brunette

MIDGE
In 1963 Barbie meets her best friend Midge. Midge is the same size as Barbie, so they can share each other's clothes.

GENUINE *Midge*® BY MATTEL®

Midge has her own special label

THEATER DATE
Barbie looks chic in emerald satin when she goes to the theater.

Pink pearl necklace

The fitted skirt has a short peplum, or overskirt

SOPHISTICATED LADY
Girls are still wearing elaborate gowns to the prom. This satin ballgown is a perfect choice.

ICEBREAKER
Midge goes skating.

1963

Barbie AND *Ken*
Teen-Age Fashion Model   Barbie's Boyfriend
and Barbie's Best Friend!™
Midge

Booklet that comes with the dolls

Silver lace

SIXTIES CHIC

A S THE SIXTIES begin to evolve, so does Barbie. The rise of youth culture leads to changes in fashion, music, and lifestyle, and Barbie captures the mood of the moment. New dolls Francie, Twiggy, and Casey arrive, dressed in "mod" fashions – Sixties-speak for modern and sophisticated.

Casual shirt and shorts for going to the beach

Frilly top and shorts for summer fun

1966

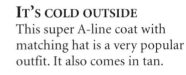

RICKY
Ricky is Skipper doll's handsome boyfriend. This is his original outfit.

SKOOTER
Skipper finds a new friend to have fun with.

IT'S COLD OUTSIDE
This super A-line coat with matching hat is a very popular outfit. It also comes in tan.

Matching hat and gold fabric clutch purse

BENDABLE LEG MIDGE
In 1965 Barbie, her friend Midge, and sister Skipper are given more lifelike legs – now they can sit and are easy to pose.

Flexible knee joints are hidden inside the legs

1965

GOLD 'N GLAMOR
This beautifully designed and constructed outfit has a real zipper, a lined tweed jacket, and furry trim on the scarf.

MAGNIFICENCE
What a glorious evening outfit! Barbie wears a vibrant coat lined in white satin, with a soft furry collar.

Decorated pink chiffon over taffeta

Tweed sheath skirt is attached to a turquoise chiffon bodice

Fully lined satin cape, with a fabulous faux fur collar

MIDNIGHT BLUE
Barbie lights up the night in an elegant ballgown in satin with a silver lamé bodice.

Bendable leg Barbie

Rare version of American Girl with a side part

AMERICAN GIRL
A new hairstyle of bangs with a center part and a short bob is introduced.

Barbie still has her sideways glance

1965

16

SUNDAY VISIT
This elegant two-piece suit is evidence that the main influence on fashion is still the couture designers.

First Lady Jacqueline Kennedy's chic suits and pillbox hats set new trends

The knit dress comes with a matching swagger jacket and a gold fabric half belt

EVENING GALA
This outfit reflects the new trend toward pants and pantsuits for women.

Real metal zipper

Gold fabric dress is lined in blue satin

Frills on the bottom of pants are very trendy

FASHION LUNCHEON
Here is an ideal outfit for having lunch at the White House! The dress has a satin bodice and matching stylish, short jacket. Elbow-length gloves, a satin hat, and a brooch add presidential touches.

Barbie can change her hair color, too!

Detachable hood

CLUB MEETING
The flowers at the waistline are made of fabric.

British pop music, led by The Beatles, takes the world by storm

NEW MODS
British pop music and stylish mod fashion are the latest craze. Francie and Casey wear this new look.

A new geometric look takes over from the twin set look

TWIST 'N TURN
This titian-haired Barbie was the doll Mattel offered in the famous exchange deal in 1967. When girls handed in an old Barbie they were given this one in return.

1966

STYLE SETTERS
Casey is a fun friend for Francie. She looks snug in this mod velvety cape with metal fasteners.

These bright flower patterns reflect current trends

TWIGGY
The first celebrity Friend of Barbie to be introduced is Twiggy, as a tribute to the top British model.

A way-out dress under a groovy plastic raincoat with a hood

CLEAR OUT!
Cousin Francie has a new straighter figure so that she can wear the mod British fashions of the day.

COLOR MAGIC BARBIE
This Barbie has hair and clothes that can change color before your eyes – it's magic!

A stylish traveling case matches the outfit

Twiggy's logo was based on her signature style of long eyelashes

The actual Twiggy steps out

1967

Barbie has an English friend called Twiggy

It's the latest idea – boots – come rain or shine!

SWINGING SIXTIES

NOW THE SIXTIES are really swinging. Skirts are even shorter and Barbie is wearing trendy minidresses and pantsuits to the go-go clubs. Her face has changed, too! She looks younger, with long eyelashes and wide blue eyes.

1968

Hot pink lace ruffles on the dress hem

This white and gold knit shift dress is totally Sixties

DANCING STRIPES
This super short shift dress and coat set is the newest fashion statement.

INTRIGUE
Is Barbie a detective or a secret agent in this slinky gold fabric trench coat?

SCENE STEALER
Party wear for Barbie is now less formal and glows with color. Here she wears contrasting pink and green.

Breezy pink coat with satin edging

Fully lined

An original designer outfit of the time

TWIGSTER
Art and fashion influence each other. Twiggy's boldly patterned dress reflects the ideas of a Sixties style called Op Art.

Looking cool with sunglasses on her head

SPARKLE SQUARES
It's the Space Age and designers turn to metallic fabrics, as in this shift and matching coat worn by red-haired Stacey.

JUMP INTO LACE
Jumpsuits are all the rage. Here new British friend Stacey wears her version – a daring outfit.

Trendy long scarf

1969

Mod fashions

FANCY DANCY
Acid chartreuse green and hot fuchsia pink collide in a mod dress and jacket.

SWIRLY CUE
Multicolored, swirling prints are typical of the late Sixties style – mind-boggling patterns are known as psychedelic.

Psychedelic pattern

TALKING PJ
Here is a new friend for Barbie called PJ. Her mod dayglo miniskirt with hotpants is groovy.

1969

Real-life dress with swirling design

TALKING BARBIE
She can speak English and Spanish and she has a new hairstyle!

1969

WALKING JAMIE
Barbie has a new friend called Jamie. She is also available with red hair.

This year dresses are very, very short

CHRISTIE
Christie is the first African-American friend for Barbie. She has ethnically correct curly brown hair, large brown eyes, and light brown skin.

Talking Christie

Her boyfriend Brad arrives in 1970, and his first words are "Christie's the greatest!"

Pull the ring to make Brad speak!

BENDABLE LEGS KEN
After a year's absence, Ken returns in 1969 with a longer hairstyle, a more trendy wardrobe, a muscular body, and more flexible legs.

Originally, Julia had dark brown hair, but it has oxidized over time

Nurse's pin

JULIA
Julia is a friend of Barbie. She is based on the popular TV character called Julia Baker, as played by Diahann Carroll.

Onepiece nurse's uniform

Matching vinyl hat

GREAT COAT
Glossy vinyl looks great and costs a lot less than leather. It is soon a popular choice for coats and jackets.

Barbie has straight, waist-length hair with uneven ends

1969

Alternative Francie hairstyles

Barbie wears orange lipstick to match her bright orange net jacket

Living Skipper is totally flexible, too!

FRANCIE
Francie has pretty hair which grows when pulled! She comes with pink pumps.

PRETTY POWER
The ruffle trimmed blouse is a new fashion. The skirt's floral swirls are part of the psychedelic look.

DRAMATIC NEW LIVING BARBIE
Introduced in 1970, this Barbie is "as full of life as you are." She can move all her joints, tilt her head, and twist and turn.

1970

FLOWER POWER

MAKING MUSIC, seeking universal peace, and exploring alternative ways of living are features of this decade. The tempo of life is slower than in the Sixties. Skirt lengths go from mini to midi then maxi. Barbie and friends wear way-out or hippy costumes, and wear their hair long and loose.

BARBIE WITH GROWIN' HAIR
Long, changeable hair is now a fashion must. This Barbie has hairpieces and accessories for every occasion.

Pink satin dress has a groovy zigzag hemline.

COUNTRY CAMPER
Young people are inspired to get back in touch with the beauty of nature. Barbie enjoys exploring the country in her way-out camper with her friends.

Ken wears a suedecloth suit and an amazing floral shirt

Busy Hands Barbie has movable thumbs so that she can actually grip things, such as this glass goblet

1972

1970

TWIST 'N TURN BARBIE
Barbie can now twist and turn in every direction wearing her new bodysuit to gymnastics class.

LIVE ACTION KEN
Ken is far-out in his funky suedecloth vest with fringes. The floral shirt is fabulous, too.

WILD BUNCH
Francie wears this ultra-short, shaggy imitation fur coat that is totally "in." Bright clashing colors show the sense of fun that fashion has at this time.

TALKING BARBIE
The third in a series of talkers, this Barbie looks glamorous in her glitzy gold fabric cover-up.

Wide suedecloth belt

Typical Seventies Afghan coat and hat

1971

LIVE ACTION ON STAGE
She dances! She's hip! On her motorized stage, Barbie grooves to the beat.

WALK LIVELY BARBIE
With her straight center-parted hair and jumpsuit, Barbie is very Seventies.

Jersey knit fabric

Shoulder bags are the latest thing and are very practical!

The Partridge Family from the TV series is a typical Seventies flower power family

MALIBU BARBIE
The year 1971 sees the introduction of Malibu Barbie, Skipper, Ken, and Francie. They are all suntanned with white-blonde hair. Very California – and extremely popular!

WALK LIVELY STEFFIE
Steffie wears this up-to-the-minute psychedelic nylon jumpsuit – she looks fab!

QUICK CURL BARBIE
Hair is very much a fashion accessory and this Barbie has hair that can be curled and styled. Tiny wires in the hair make it easier to curl.

From 1973 on, outfits for Barbie are no longer named. They are now known only by their numbers

1972

1973

Seventies clothes often have a totally coordinated look

Granny dresses with frills remain the height of fashion

SWEET SIXTEEN
This homespun-looking dress is similar to Ralph Lauren's Prairie collection in the US and Laura Ashley's Victorian look in Britain.

Ken has a selection of moustaches and sideburns to change his appearance

MOD HAIR KEN
In 1973 Ken has rooted hair for the first time. Facial hair suddenly becomes a feature for any trendy young man.

1974

Jeans are the new fashion item for seriously cool Seventies people

SKIPPER
This Skipper is sold in a bag – she is known as a baggie! All Barbie dolls sold this way are less expensive than other dolls.

SEVENTIES STYLE

A S THE SEVENTIES progress, fashion turns another corner. While Barbie wears simpler hairstyles and outfits, Ken looks more and more far-out. Long hair is still a fashion must, and the decade ends with the arrival of a new look – Superstar Barbie and Ken.

GOLD MEDAL BARBIE
1976 is an Olympic year. International athlete Barbie trains hard to compete in the Summer Games, held in Montreal, Canada.

Skipper grows taller

She's 2 dolls in 1 for twice as much fun!

Growing up Skipper

Make her grow from a young girl to a teenager in seconds!

1975

GROWING UP SKIPPER
Reflecting the current interest in teen culture, Skipper becomes a teenager before your eyes. With a twist of her arm she gets taller, her bust develops, and she has a trimmer waistline!

Gold Medal Ken is a competitor in the Winter Olympics – he competes in the downhill ski races

HAWAIIAN BARBIE
Easy air travel means that Barbie vacations in Hawaii and brings back this authentic hula costume.

Her lei (garland), grass skirt, and ukelele are typically Hawaiian

Knee-high socks

DELUXE QUICK CURL CARA
Cara is a friend of Barbie. Here she wears a country-style knitted shawl and simple frilly cotton dress as part of the "natural" look. Her hair can be curled, too.

TEN SPEEDER
As part of a new move toward personal fitness, Barbie exercises on her ten-speed bike.

1976

PARTY TIME BARBIE
Halter tops and long skirts are definitely in fashion! So are brightly colored floral prints. This outfit is available only in Europe.

A Seventies model wears a typical floral dress

1974

BUSINESS SUIT
Casual dress is worn more and more by men. This stylish beige suit with extra wide lapels is the latest thing.

Chunky shoes are still in fashion

1976

22

NOW LOOK KEN
White suits like this are all the rage, especially after John Travolta dances to fame in the movie *Saturday Night Fever*.

SUPERSIZE BARBIE
This new Barbie is very tall (18 in/450 cm). With her long, sunstreaked blonde hair and silver gown, she is beautiful and elegant.

The actors in the hugely successful TV show Charlie's Angels (above) portray women who are glamorous and dynamic – girls see them as their new role models

1978

With her long, blonde, wavy hair, Barbie is the epitome of Seventies glamor

PARTY TIME BARBIE
Barbie wears glitter and sparkle – on her lips, hair, and clothes. This doll is sold only in Europe.

STAR 'VETTE
With the disco craze at its height, Barbie can now arrive at the discotheque in style, in her new Star 'Vette car. She looks every inch the Hollywood superstar.

Ken has donned a sleek celebrity jumpsuit with belt. Notice the identity bracelet and shades.

SUPERSTAR BARBIE AND KEN
Sunstreaked hair and wide, white smiles are features of the new-look Barbie, Ken, and Christie dolls.

Superstar Christie goes dancing in this truly glamorous satin dress with matching frilly boa and strappy shoes

1979

SCOTT
Men's hairstyles are getting longer and wilder. Skipper now has a boyfriend, Scott, who sports the untamed look.

CASUAL SUIT
Relaxed styles are in – Ken even wears this red leisure suit to the office these days.

1980

SUPERSTAR!

THE GLAMOR LOOK takes off in the Eighties. No longer interested in the natural look, Barbie now enjoys being glamorous and beautiful and, of course, wearing fabulous outfits.

Legendary singer Tina Turner is a glamorous star from these years

Country and western singer Dolly Parton

BEAUTY SECRETS
Now Barbie has a complete beauty routine – she can put on lipstick, comb her hair, and brush her teeth. Push a panel in her back to make her move.

KISSING BARBIE
A doll that kisses and does not tell, Kissing Barbie puckers up and makes a kissing sound. She then leaves a mark on your cheek with her special lipstick!

1981

Twist and turn waist

MY FIRST BARBIE
This Barbie is intended for a younger age group. She has smoother legs and she's easier to dress!

GOLDEN DREAM CHRISTIE
Christie looks like a movie star in this shimmery gold outfit. She also has hair styling equipment.

Chiffon cape can be worn around the waist or shoulders

HAPPY BIRTHDAY BARBIE
Reflecting the new interest in country and western music and clothes, Barbie has an elaborately curled hairstyle.

1981

SPORT & SHAVE KEN
This Ken is a well groomed guy. He "shaves" off his water-soluble ink "beard" with a foam "razor."

Ken is ready for a shave

The stars of the popular TV show Dallas *inspire a new trend toward western-style clothes*

Afro hairstyle

BARBIE BREAKS NEW GROUND
Although Barbie has had friends from the African-American and Hispanic communities for years, 1980 sees the arrival of the first-ever African-American Barbie and the first Hispanic Barbie. Now Barbie better represents our multicultural society.

1980

DALLAS
Western Barbie has a new horse, a beautiful palomino called Dallas. This particular Barbie can wink, too!

The first Hispanic Barbie

This Barbie wears a hat and cape over pants

1982

This lovely dress has a lacy trim and a ribbon tie

Barbie wears a hot pink fluffy sweater and cowboy boots

DESIGNER DENIM
Barbie and Ken update their denims and join in the fashion craze for designer jeans.

PINK 'N PRETTY
There are over twenty ways to wear this fabulous outfit with its faux fur trim.

MAGIC CURL
Barbie has gone curly! Her hair can be straightened with a Magic Mist solution.

Miniature cameo pin

Makeup

Barbie has her own designer jeans label

ANGEL FACE
The old-fashioned prairie girl look was the inspiration for this romantic lace blouse and long satin skirt.

Her jeans are fashionably tucked into her boots

Barbie is living the life with her fabulous furniture collection

1983

ENTERTAINMENT CENTER SET
Barbie entertains in style at her home. She has a large comfortable sofa, an elegant coffee table, a pretend TV and stereo.

DREAM DATE
Barbie and Ken dress up to go out on a date.

ALL STAR KEN
These days Ken is really in shape! He works out and has the muscles to prove it. If you bend his arm his muscle pops up.

DREAM STORE MAKEUP DEPARTMENT
What fun! A makeup center just for Barbie! There is real makeup to use and a shopping bag to fill.

Hot pink tricot dress with a halter top and silvery waistband

1983

TWIRLY CURLS
This Barbie doll has a mane of hair that reaches to her mid-thigh! It can be curled with a Twirly Curler.

The set includes pretend containers, bottles, jars with tops, and a powder puff

Sunsational Malibu Barbie and Skipper enjoy their days at the beach

INTERNATIONAL DOLL

FROM FITNESS FADS to flamboyant designer clothes, in the mid-Eighties fashion trends change with astonishing speed. Women learn how to keep in shape and how to express themselves. They are career minded, yet like to look totally glamorous. It's a heady mix and Barbie looks fabulous throughout.

This soft stole can be worn in many different ways

PEACHES 'N CREAM
This chiffon gown is a pure over-the-top fashion statement – typically Eighties in style.

LOVIN' YOU
Barbie is a sweetheart of a doll in her dress covered with crimson hearts.

Barbie has a gym bag and her own exercise routine

TROPICAL BARBIE
The sun always shines for Tropical Barbie, in her single-strap bathing suit and petal skirt.

Barbie has two-toned blonde hair

1985

1985

The vest, socks, and tie Ken wears are also iridescent

CRYSTAL BARBIE
Barbie celebrates her 25th anniversary – Eighties style! She and Ken make a dazzling duo in white. Barbie has a shimmery dress and Ken an iridescent tux.

Fitness Time

Leg warmers

Barbie goes for the "burn" to keep in shape

Ribbon sash

Jane Fonda inspires women to get in shape when her ground-breaking workout video is a huge success

1984

MY FIRST BARBIE
This Barbie was the first African-American version in the My First Barbie series. What a cute dress!

GREAT SHAPE
The aerobics craze has a massive impact on fashion – leotards, leg warmers, and other workout gear are the latest look.

The Material Girl herself, Madonna is a pop star who tells women to express themselves in their clothes and hairstyles

1987

ASTRONAUT
This is part of a series of way-out outfits for Barbie called Adventures in Space. They all feature huge shoulders and have imaginative names, such as Galaxy a Go-Go.

ROCKER BARBIE
Barbie sings with her rock group dressed in these silver lamé pants and starry top.

1988

ROCKER DEE-DEE
Barbie and her friends start a group called Barbie and The Rockers. They lose their squeaky-clean image and dress like singer Madonna.

1986

JEWEL SECRETS WHITNEY
The figure-hugging dress worn by Whitney reflects that Eighties women are more confident than ever. She's dressed to impress in a sequinned gown with shiny accessories.

Glamorous singer Whitney Houston wears streamlined, sequinned gowns in concert

HAPPY HOLIDAYS
This stunning Barbie launches the Happy Holiday series in 1988.

Princess Diana's beauty and taste inspire many women to copy her style during the Eighties

DAY-TO-NIGHT
In the work-obsessed Eighties, like many women, Barbie is passionate about her career. But she finds time to play hard too. After work her stylish suit can be reversed to become a striking chiffon and lamé evening dress.

RUSSIAN DOLL
Started in 1980, the Dolls of the World series has nineteen dolls by 1989. The latest is this luxurious-looking Russian doll.

1990

Short chiffon peplum, or overskirt

PARTY PINK
Watch out, world! Barbie is set to stun in an off-the-shoulder knit party dress.

BLUE DREAM
Barbie is talking to her friends before going out to her dinner date.

PARTY 'N PLAY
Skipper wears trendy teen gear to go partying with her friends.

MY FIRST KEN FASHIONS
These four fun outfits for Ken are designed with young children in mind.

TOTALLY HAIR BARBIE AND KEN
Totally Hair Barbie has the longest hair of any doll – it is 11½ in (293 cm) long – and she is the best selling Barbie to date.

The bright psychedelic dress and shirt give this pair a retro Seventies look

1991

NINETIES BARBIE

BARBIE REFLECTS the pace of Nineties life. She drives a superb car, travels the world, and enjoys rocking and rapping. Her hair is the longest ever. She's thrilled when top fashion designers design dresses for her.

1992

FRIENDSHIP BARBIE
This Barbie is issued to celebrate the fall of the Berlin Wall in 1990.

BARBIE FERRARI
What style! This dream car suits the glamorous lifestyle of Barbie. It has a special Barbie license plate, too.

EARRING MAGIC BARBIE
This Barbie comes with star and heart charms to attach to her earrings or waist belt.

1990

BARBIE AND THE BEAT
Barbie loves to jam with her guitar and her new group called The Beat.

STACIE
Barbie has a new sister called Stacie. She is small (Tutti-sized), with thigh-length hair, and is lots of fun.

1992

Earring Magic Ken joins in with a single earring and becomes a big favorite

MOTORCYCLE KEN
In his black leather-look jacket with chain and studs, Ken is a really cool dude. Barbie can ride behind, too!

Ken doll's motorcycle is a macho red until washed, when it turns Barbie pink!

BABY SISTER KELLY
Barbie loves taking care of her cute new baby sister, Kelly.

BAYWATCH™
This doll was launched to coincide with the popular TV program and shows Barbie as a trained lifeguard.

1995

Her eyes close when they are washed

CAMP BARBIE
Here, Barbie is seen in the great outdoors with all her friends around the campfire.

DOCTOR BARBIE
This is a new career for Barbie. As a pediatrician she takes care of children.

BEDTIME BARBIE
The first doll with a fabric body, this Barbie is soft and cuddly to take to bed. Brush her teeth and her mouth closes, too.

RAPPIN' ROCKIN'
Barbie hip-hops to the boom box beat with attitude!

This life-like Barbie has makeup and jewelry that can be shared by her owner

1994

GYMNAST BARBIE
With her new bendable body, Barbie looks like a real gymnast!

1993

MC Hammer makes rap music cool in the Nineties. He is even made into a "friend of Barbie" doll

A boom box for rapping

MY SIZE BARBIE
This doll stands 3 ft (915 cm) tall, and her clothes can be worn by little girls.

BARBIE NOW!

B ARBIE REFLECTS the interests of girls everywhere. She plays hard, she rocks hard, and she can rise to any occasion with style and elegance. As Barbie enters the next millennium, she inspires a whole new generation of girls with her slogan "be anything."

WORKIN' OUT BARBIE
Barbie keeps slim and trim to music on her own cassette player and earphones. This doll has suction cup shoes to keep her steady during workouts.

SHARE A SMILE BECKY
Barbie doll's new friend Becky is in a wheelchair – this development shows the changes in attitudes toward people of different abilities.

1996

Suction cup

1997

FLYING HERO
With this wonderful magical cape, Barbie is given the powers to "fly" into action and save the world.

DENTIST
Barbie tackles a new career as a dentist. Here, she is teaching her young patient about tooth hygiene.

OLYMPIC GYMNAST
This Barbie is ultra flexible and a gold medal winner.

Multicolored braids are fun!

Dentist's chair

1998

TEEN SKIPPER
This Skipper has grown up! She has a new body shape and a real teenage look in 1997.

BEYOND PINK
The rise in popularity of all-girl bands leads to more girl pop stars than ever before. Rock on Barbie!

MOVIN' 'N GROOVIN'
This Barbie magically "walks" by herself. Her feet print out patterns as she walks. It's fun art and girls love to make lots of interesting designs.

1998

The Spice Girls are one of the most popular girl groups of the Nineties – they support the idea of "Girl Power."

SHAVE 'N STYLE KEN
With strong colors, everyday clothing, and a rugged unshaven appearance, this Ken has tons of modern appeal.

Filmstar Brad Pitt is the new heart-throb of the Nineties

WORKING WOMAN™
Executive case, diary, and mobile phone – these are essentials for today's professional woman on the go.

1999

Pink and lilac streaked hair

HAPPENING HAIR
Outrageous hair colors are exciting news. Barbie wears baggy jeans with topstitching – every teenager with a keen eye on fashion has a pair of these too.

Thick-soled sneakers

MILLENNIUM GIRL
Barbie loves this silver and purple outfit – both favorite colors at the end of the twentieth century! Her outfit shows the free-and-easy styles of the late Nineties.

Top supermodel Claudia Schiffer in a casual outfit

GENERATION GIRL
Here is Barbie with some of her new hip, teenage friends (Nichelle, Tori, Ana, and Chelsie). A fifth friend, called Lara (not pictured), is also introduced. Controversially, the first few Chelsie dolls have a nose stud, but this detail is later omitted.

Nineties supermodel Naomi Campbell

1999

BARBIE AND KRISSY
Here is Barbie proudly walking her new baby sister Krissy who arrives in 1999.

HAPPY 40TH ANNIVERSARY
Barbie celebrates her fortieth birthday in this wonderful black evening gown. Her bouquet is 40 red long-stemmed roses.

2000

BUTTERFLY ART
Modern Christie has fun washable body art stickers and wears friendship bracelets! These reflect the teenage trends of the day – they're so funky!

BARBIE PERSONIFIES THE AMERICAN DREAM

SHE OWNS HER OWN HOUSE, HER OWN CAR, HER OWN LIFE. LET'S TAKE A CLOSER LOOK.

HOME
is where the
HEART
is

2

HOME SWEET HOME

BARBIE SET UP HOME for the first time in 1961 with her portable Dream House. Made entirely out of cardboard, the house was light to carry, easy to assemble, and came complete with lots of tasteful accessories that were carefully selected by Barbie to create her ideal home.

The built-in wardrobe houses her designer outfits

Barbie looks so stylish in Sheath Sensation – her best-selling outfit from 1959 to 1963

Portable home

The entire house folds into a cardboard suitcase, complete with carrying handle.

The front of the case folds out with ease

A peek inside

The sides of the case unfold to reveal the inside of the house. No screws or attachments are required.

Pictures adorn the yellow walls

Orange louver door

Tile-effect floor

Delicate pink peignoir from Barbie doll's Nighty Negligee set

The house measures:
26 x 14.5 x 33 in
(66 x 37 x 84 cm)

Sixties chic

As to be expected from fashion-conscious Barbie, her first Dream House reflects the latest in Sixties design.

Pink dressing-table chair with cushion

Bookworm Barbie has plenty to read!

A picture of Ken adorns the cabinet shelf

Sixties-style cylindrical lamp

Built-in record player and television cabinet

Checkered blinds match the sofa

Barbie has wide-ranging tastes in music

Sixties-style sofa with red and blue checkered pattern

Coffee table

Barbie keeps cool in a butterfly-patterned dress called Coffee's On

Girl talk

The furniture can be rearranged according to taste, and there is always plenty of room for guests!

Barbie is wearing a turquoise dress suit called Club Meeting

Barbie puts her feet up with this matching blue chair and footstool.

Bed shows a cotton sheet added later

URBAN LIVING

BARBIE GETS a new Family House in 1967 that reflects the latest trends in urban design. Featuring brightly colored psychedelic patterns and curved furniture made from molded plastic, this home is as up-to-the minute as ever.

Pink plastic corrugated roof

The house measures:
13 x 13 x 9½ in
(33 x 33 x 24 cm)

the world of *Barbie* house

Brightly printed scene shows Barbie and friends relaxing by the pool

Portable fun
The house folds up into a box that is light and easy to carry.

Barbie wears an acrylic Mod outfit called Fancy Dancy (1968)

Opening up
The case opens into a colorful bedroom and living room. It's time to play house!

Yellow and orange patterned "carpet"

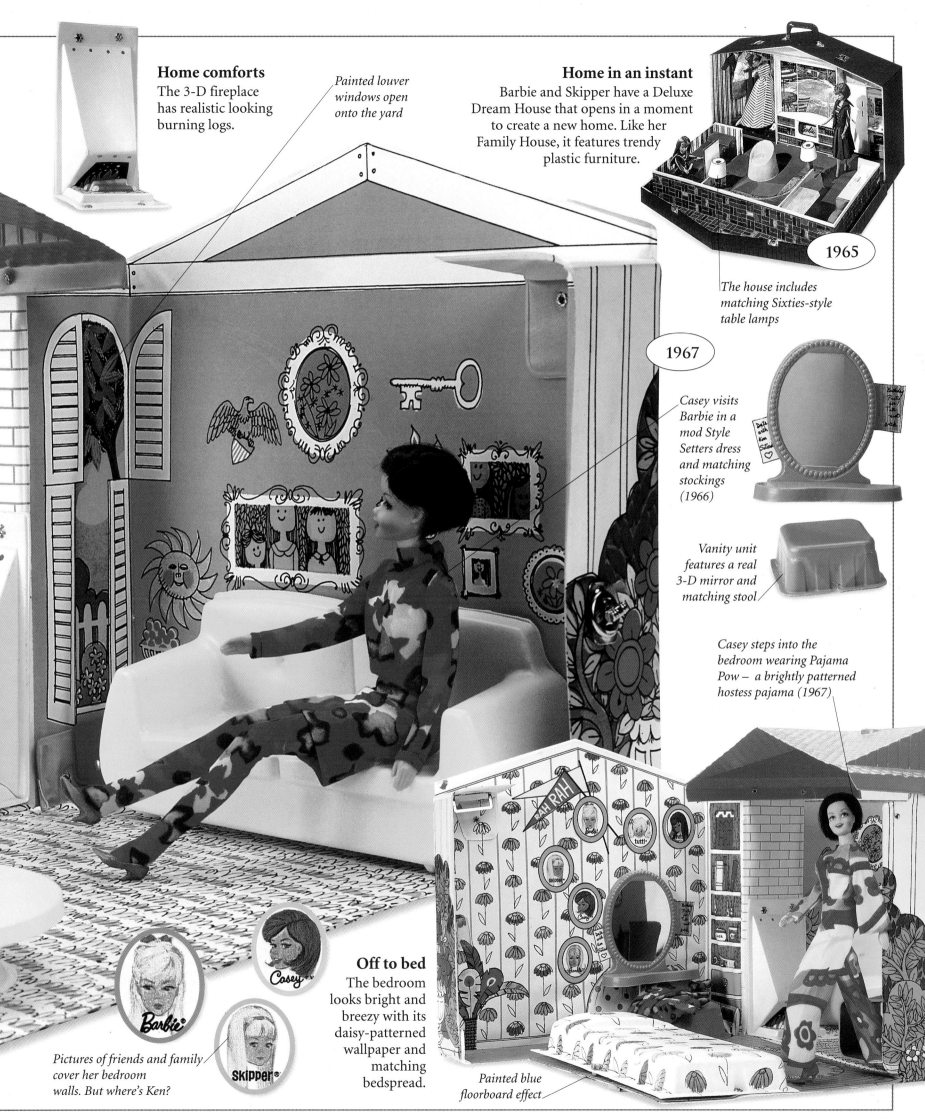

Home comforts
The 3-D fireplace has realistic looking burning logs.

Painted louver windows open onto the yard

Home in an instant
Barbie and Skipper have a Deluxe Dream House that opens in a moment to create a new home. Like her Family House, it features trendy plastic furniture.

1965

The house includes matching Sixties-style table lamps

1967

Casey visits Barbie in a mod Style Setters dress and matching stockings (1966)

Vanity unit features a real 3-D mirror and matching stool

Casey steps into the bedroom wearing Pajama Pow – a brightly patterned hostess pajama (1967)

Off to bed
The bedroom looks bright and breezy with its daisy-patterned wallpaper and matching bedspread.

Pictures of friends and family cover her bedroom walls. But where's Ken?

Casey

Barbie

Skipper

Painted blue floorboard effect

FIT FOR A PRINCESS

IN THE SEVENTIES, house styles for Barbie change from plain rustic to sophisticated city dweller. Increasingly, her home no longer reflects the fashions of the day, and by the early Nineties, Barbie creates a pink and glamorous lifestyle that is all her own.

Swinging shutter doors

Rounded tower adds to the fairytale look

1974

Stable door

Basic furniture

Country life
In the early Seventies, Barbie goes back to nature with her hippy-style Country Living home.

Downtown
Barbie moves into her Town House in 1974. This three-story townhouse features a moving elevator and rooms with photographic backdrops.

1974

Eighties elegance
Barbie moves to her chalet-style Dream House in 1979. This attractive house features a balcony, window boxes filled with plants, and windows and doors that open and close.

1979

Sturdy hardwood floors

Moving elevator

Photographic backdrop

1991

Magical mansion
In the 1990s, Barbie moves up in the world with this colonial-style Magical Mansion house.

Vanity mirror with working lights

Wood-fiber walls with sparkly finish

The house measures:
4 x 3 x 2 ft
(120 x 100 x 60 cm)

French doors

Light-up chandelier

Bay window

Deluxe dream house
Barbie stays in the pink with this enchanting, Victorian-style house of 1998.

Victorian-style sloping roof

Rose patterned "stained-glass" windows

The house measures:
29 x 9 x 28 in
(74 x 23 x 71 cm)

1998

The cream colored walls are trimmed with pale pink and seafoam green

Curved balcony with balustrade

Potted plants add a homey touch

Wood-effect paneling

Working swing for Kelly to play on!

Ornate pink pillars frame the front door

Front porch

A LOOK INSIDE

THIS 1998 BARBIE DELUXE DREAM house opens up to reveal a beautifully furnished and decorated home. With its rose-patterned wallpaper and wicker-style furniture, the decor shows off Barbie doll's great design taste.

Bathtime fun

The green built-in wash basin and cabinet drop down to reveal a luxurious bathtub. This tub really does hold water and bubbles!

Casserole dish   Strainer   Cannisters

Measuring cup

Set of plates

Basket

Water jug and glasses

Serving tray

Kitchen collection

The roomy kitchen comes complete with a range of accessories.

Cordless phone

Built-in cabinet and wash basin

THE BATHROOM

Doorway to balcony

Wicker-look nightstand

Barbie calls her friends on her cordless phone

Real fabric curtains

Dining table folds out

THE KITCHEN

Oven with pull-out extension gives extra work surface

Skipper and Ken relax in the spacious kitchen-dining room

Barbie has a pet puppy

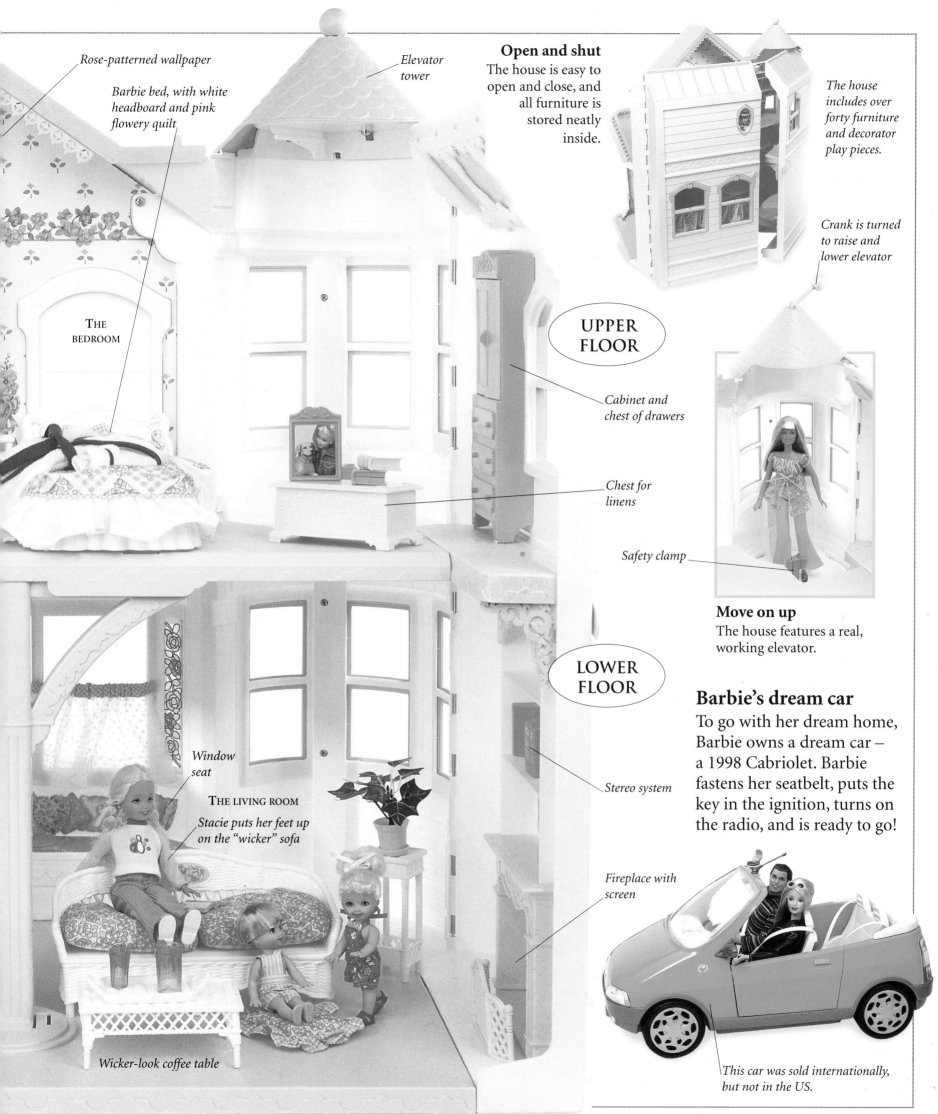

Rose-patterned wallpaper

Barbie bed, with white
headboard and pink
flowery quilt

THE
BEDROOM

Elevator
tower

Open and shut
The house is easy to
open and close, and
all furniture is
stored neatly
inside.

The house
includes over
forty furniture
and decorator
play pieces.

Crank is turned
to raise and
lower elevator

UPPER
FLOOR

Cabinet and
chest of drawers

Chest for
linens

Safety clamp

Move on up
The house features a real,
working elevator.

LOWER
FLOOR

Window
seat

THE LIVING ROOM

Stacie puts her feet up
on the "wicker" sofa

Stereo system

Fireplace with
screen

Barbie's dream car
To go with her dream home,
Barbie owns a dream car –
a 1998 Cabriolet. Barbie
fastens her seatbelt, puts the
key in the ignition, turns on
the radio, and is ready to go!

Wicker-look coffee table

This car was sold internationally,
but not in the US.

41

KITCHEN COOL

"WHAT'S COOKIN'?" asks Barbie in her 1964 apron set. In 1965, the first kitchen for Barbie arrives on the scene, and she is given a chance to show off her culinary skills. Whether it's a barbecue, picnic, or dinner for two, Barbie just loves to entertain.

1965

Dining area

Breakfast bar

Kitchen cupboards in blue and yellow

Dream kitchen-dinette

The first complete kitchen for Barbie arrives in 1965. Made from colorful particle board, the set consists of a kitchen with breakfast bar, plus dining area. Extras include a coffee percolator and toaster.

The kitchen folds away into a carrying case

Easy to hold handle

Dining table folds out from wall

Pull-down dining lamp lights up

This 1964 apron set, What's Cookin', comes complete with a chef's hat

Push-button blender really works!

Nineties Barbie pops an apple pie into the oven

Plenty of space for groceries in the kitchen cupboard

Cooking pan

Cooked

Uncooked

Pretend pizza changes color as it "cooks" in the oven!

Eating alfresco!

Barbie and friends can also eat outdoors. The outside area comes complete with barbecue and picnic table. Place the food on the barbecue, and it darkens as it cooks.

Barbecue tools

Cutting board

Table setting

1971

Shelves stacked with 3-D food and grocery packages

Country kitchen

"Country-style" living is all the rage in the Seventies, and Barbie doll's pretty, pastel-colored Country Kitchen reflects this trend. Accessories include a gingham tablecloth, "toadstool" seats, and even a fabric cat!

1975

"Toadstool" style seat with cushion

Fringed gingham tablecloth

Town and country market

Barbie loves to go shopping for her kitchen supplies! This market delicatessen is where Barbie most likes to shop. Barbie first fills her shopping cart with lots of groceries then pays at the moving check-out counter.

Cooking magic kitchen

This fabulous Nineties kitchen is described as "The Ultimate Barbie doll-sized kitchen playset" and features an outside area for barbecues and picnics.

Refrigerator with freezer

Cooking and dining

Barbie cooks and dines in style in this superb 1980s collection.

1980

Stove and oven set

Skipper helps herself to a drink from the spacious refrigerator with freezer

Refrigerator with freezer holds over thirty groceries

1991

Microwave oven

1998

Stove

Oven

Pink sparkles

Barbie goes pink with matching kitchen furnishings, including a fully functional washer and dryer.

Soapy water makes real suds and cleans Barbie doll's clothes

Motorized dryer tumbles clothes

BEAUTY TIME

FROM THE SIXTIES onward, Barbie pampers herself in a range of stylish bedrooms and bathrooms. In the early years, designs and colors vary greatly, but in the Eighties and Nineties, Barbie becomes increasingly cocooned in a fantasy world of pink.

Barbie has striped linen

Sturdy carrying handle

Striped wallpaper with flower border

Legs fold away

Barbie can enjoy breakfast in bed on her tea tray

Canopy bed
The four-poster canopy bed echoes the style of the Eighties Dream Bed shown on the opposite page.

Tricot canopy and curtains

Curtains tied with pink satin ribbons

Bedroom sofa has lift-up seat

Pampered beauty
In Bed and Bath (1998) Barbie pampers herself in her pretty pink bathroom before retiring to her luxurious boudoir.

Nightstand with alarm clock and bedside lamp

EARLY BEDROOMS AND BATHROOMS

Fantasy bedroom
These ornate, French-style bedroom furnishings appear in 1964.

Vanity unit with padded stool

1964

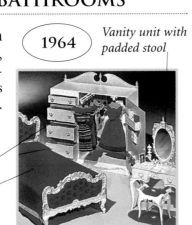

Built-in wardrobe and drawers

Queen-size bed

Barbie combs her hair by the vanity mirror

Towel rack

Frilly robe

1976

Beauty bath
The garden bathtub features a petal-shaped pump that makes the tub full of bubbles.

Cabinet for toiletries

Toilet flushes

1980

Luxury bathtub
This oval-shaped bathtub works like a real bath and comes complete with a shower head.

Bathtub with faucet

Lace pillows

Dream bed
This romantic canopy bed is a dreamy feast of ribbons, lace, and satin.

1983

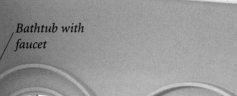

1998

Vanity stool

Wash basin with vanity mirror

Comb

Hair accessories

Hair comb

Hairdryer

Brush

Curved staircase leads to raised bathtub

Carrying case
The bedroom and bathroom fold away easily into a pretty carrying case complete with pink bow.

SWEET SECRETS

WHETHER IN PUBLIC or in private, Barbie always looks her best. In the privacy of her own bedroom, Barbie has a whole range of delicate lingerie and glamorous nightwear to change into – from satin nighties to lacy lingerie.

Barbie has her own perfume bottle

Hand mirror

Face powder and puff

Comb

MAKEUP MAGIC

Makeup box

Barbie is always perfectly groomed – and that includes her makeup!

Barbie lingerie

Barbie is a dream in this flower-patterned lingerie set from 1999.

Pink nylon stockings

Onepiece bodice with pink ribbon ties

Garter-style stocking tops

Comb

High-heeled slip-ons

Makeup bag

LEOPARD LOOK

Tiny ribbon straps

Leopard-look stretch knit (tricot) slip

Ribbon-tie belt

Matching sheer short wrap

High-heeled mules

Black lace trim

PRETTY IN PINK

Bedjacket with three-quarter length sleeves

White eyelet edging

White eyelet

Pink ribbon

Matching mules

Matching bra and panties set

DELICATE PEIGNOIR

Satin cuff

Delicate chiffon-like peignoir

High-heeled slip-ons

Satin-look ribbon

Rose-patterned nightdress

Matching hair brush

SEA-BLUE SURPRISE

Sparkly petticoat in gauze

Decorative pink bow

High-heeled slip-ons

Lacy bra with rose detail

Matching panties

LINGERIE SETS

Ribbon straps

Pretty daisy pattern

Matching slippers

Violet ribbon straps

Lace edging

White ribbon straps

Camisole and panties in brushed cotton

SIXTIES LINGERIE

This Floral Petticoat (1959–1963) is the perfect design for the full-skirted dresses that Barbie loves to wear! The delicately embroidered petticoat is worn with matching panties and bra.

Full-skirted petticoat

Stuffed dog made of pink felt

This Nighty Negligee Set (1959–1964) has a tricot gown with Grecian bodice under a matching ribbed peignoir with sheer sleeves.

STREETWISE ...
STYLISH ... SOPHISTICATED ...
HERE BARBIE OPENS THE DOOR TO HER
WARDROBE AND TO OUR IMAGINATIONS.

FASHION *and* FANTASY

3

SPRINGTIME STUNNERS

S PRING IS HERE and Barbie is ready
to step outside – dressed in bright
and breezy dresses or casual shirts
and pants. Whether having
a picnic or walking in the
countryside, Barbie always
looks as pretty as a peach.

*Halter
top*

*Fresh daisy
and check
design*

*Matching lime
green pumps*

Daisy chain
Today's Pretty in Plaid
Barbie comes in
a Sixties retro-
style minidress.

*Barbie doll's
picnic basket*

Tulle scarf

Bubble purse

*Platform
sandals*

CITY PRETTY-GREEN

*This outfit has a
cropped jacket in
ribbed chiffon*

Bell-shaped, floral cotton dress

Trendy box purse

*Strappy
stilettos*

*Straw hat to
keep off the sun*

SPRING BACK

Barbie goes fishing in her
Picnic Set (1959–61). This fun
outfit features a bright check
shirt worn with pedal
pushers, and comes
complete with a
fishing rod.

*Woven picnic
basket*

Cork wedges

Quick Curl Cara doll's dress
(1976) has a Seventies style
gathered bodice and frilled
hem. The fringed shawl and
beaded necklace add to the
peasant girl look.

*This Sixties bob is known
as American Girl*

Barbie is ready for
spring in her Fashion
Editor outfit of 1966.
The floral pattern on the
silky bodice reflects the
flowery design on the
Nineties bell-shaped
dress shown above.

PURPLE PROSE

Sheer shirt worn over a sleeveless vest top

Fitted flock skirt

Matching purse with flower motif

Knee-length skirt

Slip-on wedgies

GREEN THUMB

Denim collar and cuffs

Patterned cotton shirt

Cotton overalls

Thick cotton fabric

Fork and trowel

Wide-brimmed straw hat

Barbie works in the garden in her Green Thumb outfit complete with gardening gloves, tools, and a protective straw hat.

Protective gloves

Comfortable clogs

KEEP COOL

Long boot cut checkered pants

TOO COOL

Capped sleeved T-shirt with logo

Large box purse with clasp

Sleeveless quilted jacket

Chunky platform shoes

Hat with upturned brim

Easter chic
Barbie celebrates Easter in this special outfit of 1998. The sleeveless minidress has a daisy-chain belt.

Easter basket

SPRING PICNIC

IT'S A PERFECT spring day, and Barbie and friends are enjoying a picnic out in the countryside. While the young kids run off to play, Barbie and Ken are content to sit back and unwind. "This is bliss," sighs Barbie, "I could stay out here forever!"

Casual Ken
Ken is cool and laid-back in his cotton checked shirt and safari-style shorts.

Sun hat with upturned brim

Ken lies back and listens to the music on his CD player

Leather-look belt

Leather-look heavyweight boots

Pretty floral pattern with extra sparkle!

Barbie has made her own CDs

Jelly sandals

Barbie doll's terrier wants attention!

Island vacation
Barbie looks like a fresh spring day in her flowery blue halter dress.

Picnic set
Barbie has everything organized in her pink hamper packed with goodies!

"Wicker" hamper with lift-up lid

Daisy covered cloth

Springtime Skipper
Skipper always has her eyes on the latest fashions. She looks so cool in this stretchy T-shirt and miniskirt.

Daisy motif

Zigzag pattern

Chunky platforms

Toddler Tommy
"Where's Stacie going?" wonders Tommy, Ken's little brother, as he toddles along in his striped bib and suspenders outfit.

Bib and suspenders

Stacie
Stacie runs off to play in her brightly colored top and pants.

Bowling motif

T-shirt with fun flower motif

Pretty flowers and shapes pattern

Cool kid
Kelly has fun outdoors wearing her favorite T-shirt and top.

Sneakers are great for play

53

ON VACATION

SUMMER HAS ARRIVED and it's vacation time. Barbie packs plenty of swimsuits, sundresses, and casual shorts into her stylish matching luggage. She's ready to catch some fun in the sun with her friends wearing these pretty outfits and coordinating accessories.

DENIM SUIT

Gold fabric piping

Contrasting topstitching

Gold lamé beach bag

GLAM 'N GOLD

Anchor motif

Golden mules

Belt and buckle

Beach beauty
With such a slim figure, Barbie can wear any of these tiny bikinis or a stunning onepiece costume.

Plaid luggage

Luggage labels with initials

BANANA BELLE

Knitted fabric

Silver and blue rope strap

Tie at back

High leg bikini bottom

Brief bikini bottom

Ribbon trim

Cute matching sunhat

COUNTRY COTTON

Fresh cotton look

Daisy decoration

Short and sweet hemline

Makeup case

High-heeled pumps

DASH OF DENIM

Denim bra look

Unusual pattern

Matching purse

High-heeled slip-ons

54

EVERYDAY DENIM

CANDY CUTE

Daisy sun top

Patterned waistband on skirt

Loafers

Denim vest

Tennis shoes

All decked out
When traveling, Barbie wears this stylish outfit from the Barbara Millicent Roberts Collection (1997).

Chic blazer with metal buttons

Pretty floral skirt

ACCESSORIES

Scarf

Necklace with anchor emblem

LEMON LOVELY

Lemon crop top

US passport

Flatties

Bermuda shorts

Coordinating clutch purse with shoulder chain

Weekend case

ON THE BEACH

Barbie has always loved the beach. Here, Hawaiian Barbie (1975) wears a pretty floral bikini, matching sarong skirt, and a *lei* (garland) of flowers.

Nylon skirt

With her golden tan, Malibu Barbie (1971) is a Californian beauty in this onepiece swimsuit.

LIME 'N LILAC

Purple star decoration

Purple jelly shoes

Beige twill pants

Stylish navy and white brogues

Purple grapes motif

FUN IN THE SUN

GOLDEN SANDS and a sparkling blue sea greet Barbie on the first day of her vacation. "This is paradise," sighs Barbie as the friends gather for surfing, boating, or simply soaking up the sun, dressed in their sensational summer fashions.

Laid-back Ken
Ken is ready to go surfing in his sleeveless T-shirt and matching flower patterned shorts.

Barbie doll's fun watercraft comes complete with lifejacket and seatbelt for extra safety

Wicker-style bag and hat with flower motif

Stick-on transfers

Boogie board

Chunky sandals, perfect for the beach

Cute Kelly
Kelly looks so cute in her yellow swimsuit and pink jelly sandals. A visor helps keep the sun off.

Florida vacation Barbie
Barbie is all set for the beach in her Florida swimsuit with leopardskin patterned front.

Surfing style

Looking cool and relaxed, Florida Vacation Steven is ready to go windsurfing. Barbie doll's Windsurfin' Fun set comes with a detachable base and sail.

Dazzling day

"Hi Barbie!" calls Midge, wearing her wraparound Floatin' 'N Cool twopiece in vivid pink.

Strappy top with glitter trim

Kira loves to wear friendship bracelets!

Drawstring shorts

Cool and casual

Kira opts for a hippy-chic look with her crocheted halterneck top and denim wrapover skirt.

Sunseeker

Christie relaxes in the sun wearing her Hawaiian halterneck swimsuit with frilled bottom.

FALL FASHIONS

BARBIE DOLL'S fall fashions echo the colors of the season, with their rich reds, yellows, and browns. Jackets of leather and faux fur protect Barbie from biting winds, while vinyl raincoats keep out the rain. But whatever the weather, Barbie is always sure to shine!

Trendy sunglasses

LEATHER LOOK

Leather-look jacket – a fashion must for today

Knitted hat keeps Barbie doll's ears warm

Lime-green skirt contrasts well with black and matches jacket stitching

Ankle boots are both fashionable and practical

FURRY LOOK

Faux fur jacket with leopardskin pattern

Striking red scarf

Wraparound top

Clasp purse

Golden strap

Boot-cut pants are flattering and modern

Corduroy miniskirt

Woolen pantyhose keep legs warm

Paper purse in matching design

Corduroy cool

Barbie doll's Corduroy Cool outfit (1999) uses a clever combination of tones and textures, with warm burgundy offset by pale blue, and fabrics of corduroy and wool.

Shiny leather-look purse with furry flap

Ankle boots

Ankle boots with faux fur border

Leather-look ankle boots

Bright three-quarter length plastic raincoat is guaranteed to keep Barbie warm and dry!

Suedelike collar keeps neck warm

Matching rainhat

AUTUMN GIRL

Bright, plastic coats first became popular in the Sixties. Francie doll's straight figure is perfect for this 1966 Clam Diggers outfit – the jacket is worn with clamdiggers (culottes).

Frog fasteners

Empire-waist dress with orange plastic belt

This Snake Charmers (1970) costume looks so cool on Francie. The fake snakeskin coat is edged in faux fur trim and has a cute hat to match.

Mid-calf boots

CITY SLICKER

Sou'wester with back flap to keep rain off the neck

Tartan lining

Stretchy tops are fashionable and easy to wear

STEPPING OUT

Casual zipper jacket

Two-tone shopping purse

"Lace-up" ankle boots

Tartan umbrella

Long, straight woolen pants

Leggings, a must for any girl's wardrobe

Gathered waist with feature bow

Waterproof jacket

SKIPPER PAST AND PRESENT

Skipper doll's Sixties trenchcoat is perfect for wet days, and comes complete with umbrella and rainhat.

Nineties Skipper prefers a more casual look with her short jacket and denim skirt.

Plastic purse

Warm socks

Sneakers

White plastic boots, a fun Sixties trend

Round purse

Chunky calf-length boots

FALL GOLD

IT'S A PERFECT FALL DAY. The air is crisp and clear, and the leaves are turning red, gold, and brown. Barbie and Ken are taking their two Dalmatian dogs for a walk. "Come on pup!" calls Barbie, running ahead. "See if you can catch me!"

Red velvet
Barbie is free to roam through fall leaves in her red velvety overalls worn over a sprig-patterned stretchy top.

Pet lover
Barbie is a real pet lover, and here are two of her favorite dogs – a Dalmatian and her cute little puppy!

Barbie wears her hair long and loose

Velvety peaked cap

Dalmatian puppy has a squishy body – perfect for cuddling!

Soft, velvety overalls

Sneakers are great for long walks!

Casual Ken

Ken faces the bracing fall winds dressed in a brown and blue striped sweater worn with navy-blue corduroy pants.

Detachable collar

Soft "furry" body

Corduroy pants

Heavy-duty walking boots

WINTER WARDROBE

THE TEMPERATURE is dropping and there's a hint of snow in the air. Barbie wraps up warmly in these winter outfits for some outdoor fun. Whether in practical fleeces or glamorous faux fur, Barbie always looks good!

Matching visor protects the eyes in snowy conditions

Silvery backpack purse

MISTY MAUVE

Soft fluffy purse

Mauve satin coat has silvery buttons

Furry trim for extra comfort

Silvery belt and buckle

PINK PUFF

Lime green zipped jacket

Silvery mittens keep hands toasty warm

White ankle boots

Imitation fur trim

Double breasted satin jacket

Ski boots

Satin pants

Cute heart-shaped purse

Warm and practical ski pants

Snow Chic
Barbie looks cool and trendy in her Snow Chic-So-Chic outfit of 1998.

Pretty pink shoes

WINTERS PAST

This stylish Winter Holiday outfit (1959–1963) features a leather-look car coat with red fleecy lining for extra warmth. The striped top has a hood to keep her ears warm.

Vinyl gloves

Plaid vinyl bag

Stretch pants

Cork wedgies

Gold chain as belt

Barbie keeps cosy in her Plush Pony costume (1969), with its faux fur coat and matching miniskirt

Contrasting zingy orange vinyl trim

FURRY AND FUN

Imitation fur collar

Vinyl coat is waterproof

Russian-style furry hat

Elegant umbrella

Imitation fur wrist cuffs

WINTER WARMER

Fluffy fur trim

Silvery braid trim

Blue and white always looks cool

WINTER FUN

High lace-up boots

Fleecy top for extra warmth

Earmuffs protect Barbie from the cold

DIVA

Faux fur purse

Imitation ocelot fur looks luxurious

Fleecy mittens

It's great fun to go sledding in the snow!

Barbie can choose between purple or white boots

Nylon snow pants made from windbreaker-type material

High heeled boots

WINTER WONDERLAND

THE AIR IS CRISP AND CLEAR as Barbie and friends head for their vacation chalet set high up in the snowy alpine hills. "This place is magic," says Ken to Steven, but Barbie is looking forward to a hot drink in front of a roaring fire!

Ski hat keeps Ken doll's ears warm

Winter warmer
Steven is all set for tobogganing in his chunky knit sweater and denim jeans.

High-necked zipper top keeps out the chilly winds

Colorful geometric patterning

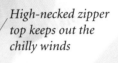

Snowflake motif

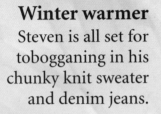

Snow sport
Ken wraps up warm in his brightly colored ski top and matching hat, worn with nylon ski pants.

Toboggan

Sturdy boots with a strong grip – perfect for the snow

Ice maiden

Christie looks simply sensational in this retro Sixties-style leather-look coat with furry trim.

Snowy-white coat with furry trim

Matching furry purse

Matching furry purse

White leggings

Blue frost

Barbie keeps warm and stays as sophisticated as ever in this gorgeous ice-blue furry coat teamed with check pants

Check pants

Snow-white boots

Chunky boots

DISCO GIRLS

BARBIE AND SKIPPER are getting ready for a night out at a dance club. But with so many exciting outfits to choose from, it's hard to decide what to wear! Should they go for a pretty, short dress or a long, elegant look?

PINK FLAPPER

Silver and pink sparkly dress

Matching clutch purse

Fringe looks great when dancing

Hot pink dancing shoes

Huge puffy sleeves

LOVELY IN LILAC

Lilac tight-fitted bodice

Shiny purple purse

Layers of sparkly tulle

Lilac stilettos

LADY IN RED

Gold brocade bodice

Evening clutch purse

Blazing red flouncy skirt

EARLY DANCING DAYS

Barbie hits the dance floor in 1968 wearing her stunning Dancing Stripes outfit. The Twenties-style sheath dress features golden straps and a lacy hemline.

Hot pink pumps

Christie's sparkly satin dress with its long frilly boa epitomizes the glamor years of the Seventies.

Matching high heels

BLUE HEAVEN

Sapphire minidress with silvery swirls

Super two-tone gold fabric party dress with a big collar

Scarlet strappy heels

GORGEOUS IN GOLD

Evening purse

Fashionable evening purse in matching fabric

Stylish blue shoes

White shoes

Disco makeup

Barbie likes to wear extra makeup under those bright disco lights. She puts on eyeliner, mascara, and a shimmery crimson lipstick.

Brown eyeliner

Small twists of hair give Barbie a new look

Vivid crimson lipstick

Fluffy wrap is worn as a bodice

Day to night

Barbie can transform her dress into a number of stunning looks – including a glamorous dress for dancing.

Hollywood Nails Barbie has blue nail polish on her fingernails!

Shiny slip-on shoes

Yo-Yo Skipper

Skipper wears a light blue T-shirt dress for daytime. The strappy minidress and shoes shown below come with the outfit.

Long skirt has slits at the side for easy movement

Chunky high-top boots for daytime

Funky sneakers for dancing

PINK SHIMMER

Silvery buckle

Glitter purse

Sharp white shoes

White pantyhose

SHORT AND SWEET

This minidress has sparkles

High pink slip-ons

TRENDY TWINSET

Long stretchy skirt

Short crop top

Cool shades

67

DANCING QUEEN

IT'S FUN TO GO DANCING! Here, Barbie and friends light up the night, movin' and groovin' to the beat. "Boogie on down Barbie!" says Ken. Anything goes in today's club scene, and Barbie is a star in her long clinging dress.

Sweet steppin'
Steven hits the floor in casual shirt and jeans. He looks great and the music is a blast.

Tricot top with straps

Matching shoulder purse

Lots of shiny circles reflect the lights

Platform sandals

Patterned scarf

Slinky dress can be worn long or short

Shining silver
Midge gleams and glistens under the disco lights in her shiny minidress.

Ice dancer
Teresa keeps her cool in ice-blue satin pants.

Happy times
Christie wears a soft tube dress that is great for energetic dancing. What a mover!

Sparkly platform shoes

Starry night
This slinky number is one of the many looks that make up Barbie doll's gorgeous outfit.

Blue boogie
Shave 'n Style Ken wears a trendy goatee beard. "Dance with me Barbie," says Ken.

White T-shirts are always in fashion

Pink sparkle
Courtney keeps cool under the hot disco lights in this halterneck minidress

Halter dress

Teen dream
Skipper grooves to the beat in her favorite sparkly, strappy minidress.

Star design in silver

Sheer wrap

Delicate chiffon-look scarf

Apricot sparkle

Matching mules

Purple poise
Look at Kira in this fabulous evening outfit called NY Night. She looks so sophisticated.

Sleek pumps

*"Silver" beaded
necklace and
matching earrings
and bracelet
complete the outfit*

*Matching
clasp purse*

Out
ON THE TOWN

Barbie and friends are enjoying a fun day out in New York City! After a morning spent sightseeing, they are hitting the stores. "How about a cappuccino, girls?" says Barbie. "These bags are beginning to get heavy!"

*Black
seamed
pantyhose*

*Black pumps
with square toe*

Glamor girl
Up-to-the-minute Christie steps out in a faux leopard-skin wraparound minidress.

*Black seamed
pantyhose*

Black pumps

Perfectly suited
Barbie is the ultimate city slicker in her satin-finish, lilac suit worn over a black bodysuit.

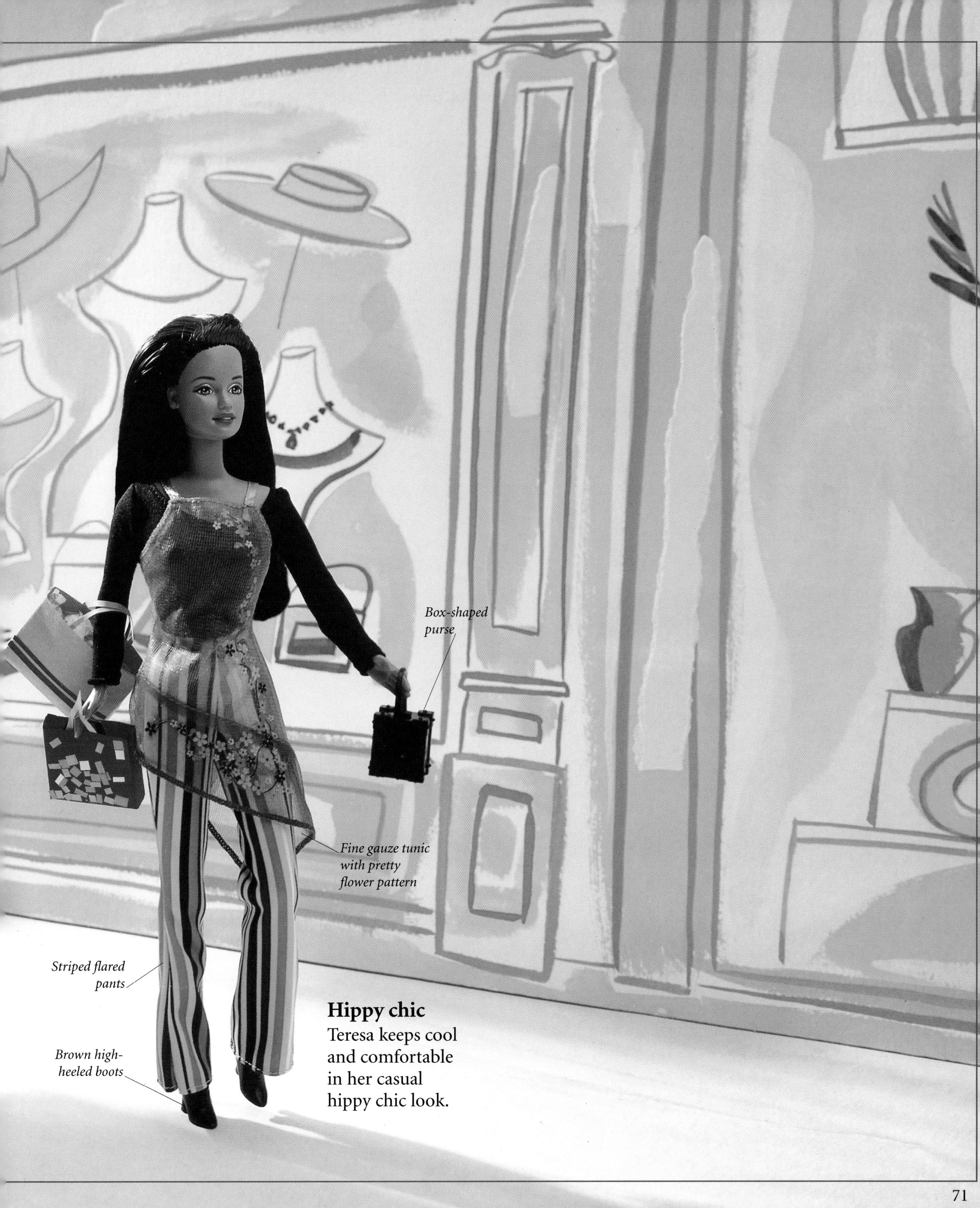

Box-shaped
purse

Fine gauze tunic
with pretty
flower pattern

Striped flared
pants

Brown high-
heeled boots

Hippy chic
Teresa keeps cool
and comfortable
in her casual
hippy chic look.

CITY GIRL

BARBIE KNOWS that suits are not the only style to be worn around town. Often fun rather than formal, her choice of city clothes includes casual jackets and pants, short and snappy miniskirts, and big-collared coats for those cold, cold days.

CITY PAST

Barbie visits London in her London Tour outfit of 1966–67. Her ecru double-breasted coat is made from vinyl.

Beret

Chiffon scarf

Fastened with four large buttons

Matching purse and shoes

Yellow vinyl purse

Suede double belt

Walk Lively Barbie roams around town in the early Seventies in a red tricot pantsuit.

Red chunky shoes

TRENDY TIE-DYE

Tie-dye top with flared sleeves

Pink, fluffy faux fur collar

Shiny plastic jacket

Blue leather-look skirt and matching purse

Platform sandals

CITY CHIC

Lime green jacket with three-quarter length sleeves

Flowery crop top

Black box purse

Black flared pants with green stitching

Black leather-look high-heeled boots

CITY JUNGLE

Zebra-patterned flared pants

Ankle boots

WOVEN WONDER

False pocket

Sheer nylon scarf

"Gold" chain and buttons

Twopiece suit in woven check fabric

Pink velveteen bag with "gold" fastener and chain

Pink pumps

CHECK-MATE

Purple and white cotton suit

Pink high-heeled ankle boots

Matching pink shoulder purse

White pantyhose

Pink and white plastic raincoat-dress

WINTER WARMER

Fringe collar

Full-length, wraparound tweed coat

Knee-high boots

Black shiny belt with big buckle

PLUM AND PRETTY

Sunglasses

Coat with faux fur collar

Striped dress with high neck

High-heeled boots

THE PURSE CLOSET

Barbie has lots of purses for days – and nights – in the city

• DAY PURSES •

Imitation fur

Leather-look

Fun "bubble" purses

GLITZY NIGHT •

Pouch purse

Lilac sparkle

Heart-shaped purse

Silver and purple clasp purses

• ENVELOPE CLUTCHES •

Gold sparkle

Midnight velvet

Pretty in pink

Cool Kira
Kira looks so chic in this turquoise two-piece called Country Club Lunch – it's the perfect outfit for any wedding, too.

Bridal "bouquet"

Pretty geometric pattern

Delicately patterned gauze worn over silken underdress

Matching clogs

Open-toed platforms

BRIDE TO BE?

B ARBIE AND FRIENDS are having fun trying on bridal outfits in an exclusive boutique. The girls sigh when Barbie emerges in a dazzling dream of a dress. "Someday..." dreams Barbie.

Party in pink
Skipper can make believe she's a bridesmaid in this delicate Barbie empire-line minidress.

Pink charmer
Christie looks so sophisticated in this sleeveless dress that has a cropped jacket. It's called Tea in London.

Dream bride
Barbie is a dream in this lacy, white bridal gown.

Full veil held in place with silvery tiara

Lady in lilac
Midge is more than happy to be maid of honor in this elegant, lilac gown.

Black ribbon bow

Gauze overskirt

Elegant pumps

Lacy overskirt

Flower girl
Kelly is having fun pretending to be a flower girl. Her cute dress is a miniature version of Midge doll's gown.

75

BLUSHING BRIDE

EVERY YOUNG GIRL dreams of her wedding day, and Barbie is no exception. Although Barbie and Ken have been together for many years, they have yet to tie the knot officially. Every season, a new wedding outfit appears in Barbie doll's wardrobe – when will her big day arrive?

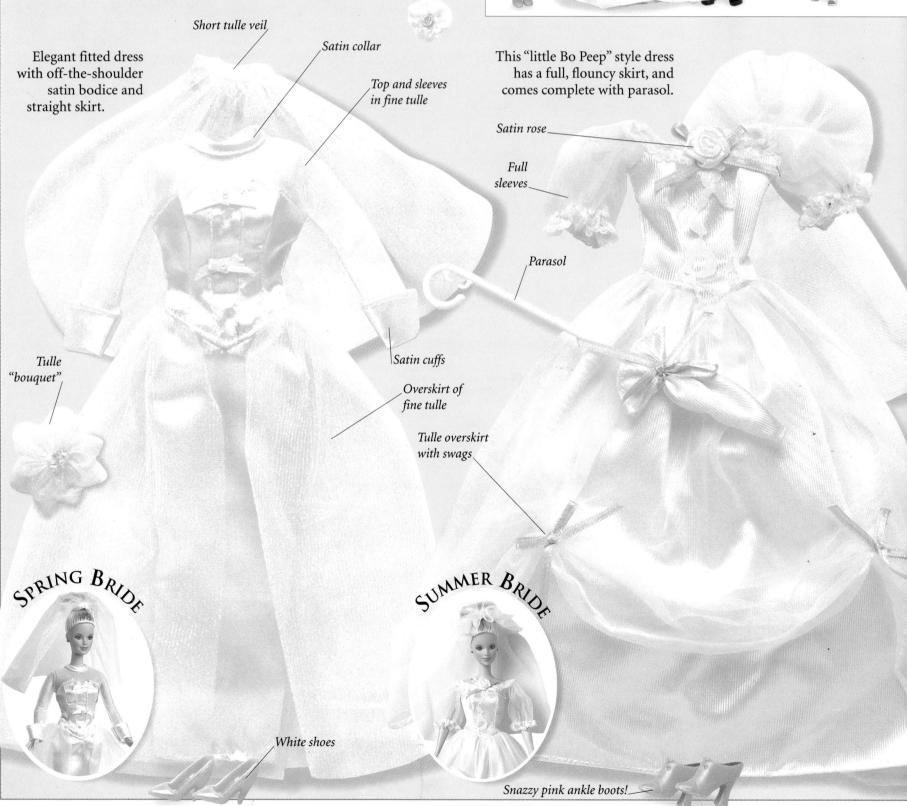

Bridesmaid Skipper

Midge is maid of honor

Short tulle veil

Satin collar

Top and sleeves in fine tulle

Elegant fitted dress with off-the-shoulder satin bodice and straight skirt.

This "little Bo Peep" style dress has a full, flouncy skirt, and comes complete with parasol.

Satin rose

Full sleeves

Parasol

Tulle "bouquet"

Satin cuffs

Overskirt of fine tulle

Tulle overskirt with swags

SPRING BRIDE

SUMMER BRIDE

White shoes

Snazzy pink ankle boots!

FOREVER LOVE

Barbie looks lovely in this Wedding Party Gift set from 1964. The gown is of white satin and chiffon, with a tiered overskirt of tulle. The bodice, with its rounded neckline and simple capped sleeves has a Sixties look. Accessories include long, white gloves. Skipper and Midge look pretty, too, in matching lemon cotton dresses with lacy overskirts.

Barbie doll's fabric bouquet

Long gloves are popular in the Sixties

Bridegroom Ken

Ken has no prewedding nerves as he steps out in his tuxedos, from fitted, Sixties style to today's informal look.

Sixties groom

Ken arrives at the church in a satin-lined jacket and pants, with burgundy bow tie and matching cummerbund (sash).

Sixties style narrow pants

Glitter groom

Ken doll's shimmering Nineties tuxedo comes complete with a dress shirt, pink bow tie, and buttonhole.

Sophisticated velveteen dress with furry jacket and hat – perfect for those cool fall days.

Fitted bodice with straps

Furry hat attached to veil

This luxurious dress in ivory is perfect for winter weddings.

Furry collar

Puffy sleeves

Golden snowflake

Jacket with furry neckline

Furry cuffs

Stretchy jersey fabric

Velvet bow

Tulle "bouquet" with snowflake

FALL BRIDE

White shoes

WINTER BRIDE

Cream ankle boots

WHAT SHALL I WEAR?

B ARBIE IS GETTING READY for a very special evening – she has been invited to a glamorous party! Barbie has to choose what to wear from a wide range of wonderful, glitzy outfits from sparkling short dresses to long and lovely evening gowns.

CHINA GIRL

Silken Asian-style tunic and capri pants

Mandarin collar

Capped sleeves

Deluxe extras

Matching evening purse

Capri pants

High-heeled sandals

NIGHT OUT

This shimmering silver dress with flared skirt is perfect for dancing

Gauze top

Silver buckle

Matching purse with silver buckle detail

Elegant v-throat shoes

Full satin cape with faux fur collar

SIXTIES STYLE

Barbie will go to the ball in this stunning Midnight Blue ensemble of 1965. The blue satin cape is worn over a strapless silver lamé bodice and full satin skirt.

Barbie looks so elegant in her Evening Gala outfit of 1966. The silver and gold overdress can be worn over bell-bottom pants, as shown, or over a full-length satin skirt.

Picture hat decorated with red satin roses

Silver and gold brocade overdress

Satin bell-bottom pants fringed with chiffon

Turquoise satin lining

Clear, open-toed sandals

Silver lamé sheath dress

Red satin coat with dropped waist

Ankle-strap shoes

Barbie is set to shine in her 1966 Shimmering Magic evening outfit which features an outrageous white organdy picture hat.

DREAM DATE

Short, halter dress in sparkling silver and purple

Fine gauze scarf

Matching purse with silver strap

Frilled hemline

GOLDEN GLOW

Golden fabric

Faux fur collar and cuffs

Long evening gloves

Faux fur wrap with golden lining, a glamorous alternative for cold nights

Long and lovely

For that very special evening, full-length evening gowns give an added touch of glamor.

Golden fabric

Ribbon-bow fastener

Golden shoes with buckle

Brown box purse

Lady in red

Barbie is now ready to leave for the party, dressed in a full-length hooded cape coat in satin.

Luxurious full-length evening coat in leopard print with gold sparkle

Flouncy off-the-shoulder satin sleeves

SOPHISTICATED LADY

Necklace with silvery pendant

Fitted full-length velvet skirt with silver sequins

Satin gloves

Black velvet evening purse with sequins

High-heeled sandals with ankle straps

GLAMOROUS NIGHT OUT

B ARBIE AND FRIENDS have been invited to a glamorous summer ball, and there is a sense of anticipation in the air as the girls (and Ken) prepare to make their entrance. "Come on, guys, let's join the fun," says Barbie. "This should be a night to remember!"

Golden girl
Resplendent in a tightly fitted gold and pink dress, Teresa greets Barbie.

Blue sparkle
Christie looks simply stunning in this shimmering, satin-look gown.

Elegant evening jacket

Black-rimmed glasses

Silvery dots change color when they reflect the light

Matching purse

Full, flowing satiny skirt

Golden clutch purse

Swirl pattern of gold, crimson, blue, and purple

Gorgeous fluffy feather boa

Cool dude
Ken looks so cool in his 1998 black tuxedo, complete with gray patterned cummerbund and bow tie.

Black rose

Barbie is the belle of
the ball in this black
off-the-shoulder dress,
with the pink, glittery
overskirt lending a
dramatic touch.

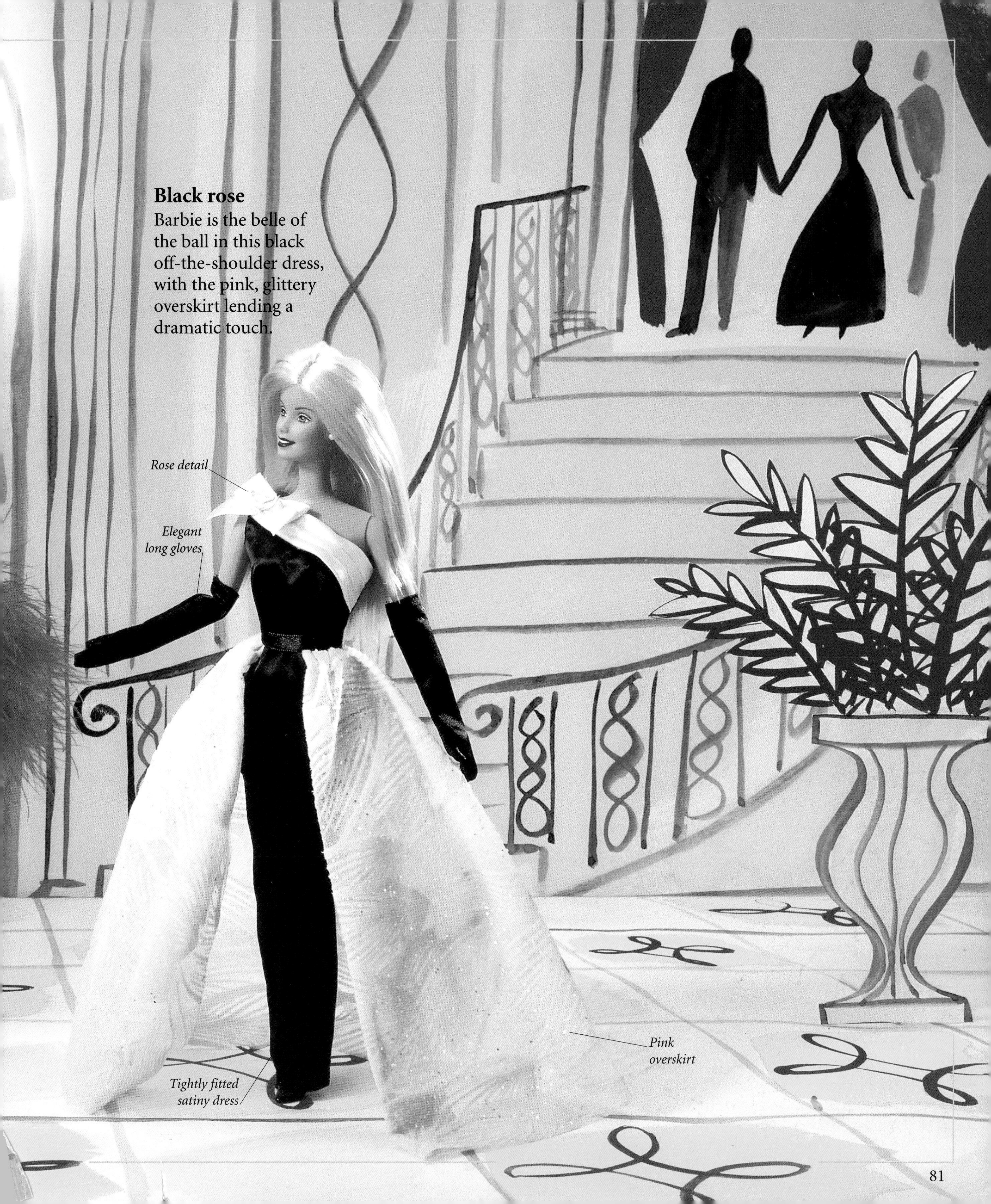

Rose detail

*Elegant
long gloves*

*Pink
overskirt*

*Tightly fitted
satiny dress*

Barbie is Continually Expanding Her Versatile and Limitless Roles to Inspire Girls' Dreams

Here Are a Few of Her Many Incarnations.

Be
ANYTHING

4

THE COLLECTIBLES

FROM THE MID-EIGHTIES, collectible and limited edition dolls begin to appear. With their stunning costume design and exquisite attention to detail, these dolls appeal to Barbie fans of all ages.

Happy Holidays series

A series of dolls designed to celebrate the holidays, the Happy Holiday collection was launched in 1988. The first doll retailed at around US$25–30, but its collector value today is up to US$850.

Happy Holidays (1998)

The last in the series, Barbie goes out in style with this velvety gown of black and silver. A satin-lined stole with tassels at each end completes the look.

Happy Holidays (1990)

This Happy Holidays doll is resplendent in ivory satin with sparkly edging and tulle underskirt. The doll's "ruby" necklace and red ribbon add a contrasting touch.

Pink splendor

Limited to only 10,000 dolls worldwide, this breathtaking creation is one of the Ultra Limited series of dolls that have been produced in very small numbers.

Hair is braided and coiled high on head

Long drop crystal earrings

Bodice made of golden lace over pale pink taffeta, studded with rhinestones

Gold-edged ribbon

Fine silk satin gown trimmed with delicate, glittering lace

Millennium princess

Created to celebrate the new millennium, this magnificent doll is dressed in a royal blue velvety gown. The doll comes complete with a "crystal" ball.

Tiara

High collar of lace and organza

Front panel of shimmering organza and silvery glitter lace

Patriot Barbie

Dressed in a rich red gown and navy military-style jacket, Patriot Barbie looks back to the American Revolution of the 18th century.

Tricorne hat

Golden liberty bell

Headband with feather plumes

Twenties-style bobbed hair

Feather boa

Beaded necklace

Dance 'till dawn

Here Barbie celebrates the "Roaring Twenties" in this lavender "flapper" dress, one of the Great Fashions of the 20th Century series.

Train adorned with pink roses

Decorated hip sash

Ruffled tiered bottom

FANTASY DOLLS

ENTER THE FANTASY world of Barbie and let your imagination run free with these stunning collectible dolls. These delightful designs reflect a dream world of angels, birds, and flowers.

Headdress topped with feathers and rhinestones

Flowing, layered gown in flamingo-pink

Flamingo

This wonderful doll appears in the fanciful Birds of Beauty Collection. Flamingo Barbie celebrates the tropical bird in real style.

Harpist angel

The first doll in the Angels of Music Collection, this enchanting Barbie has feather wings and holds a golden stringed harp.

Delicate feather wings

Periwinkle chiffon gown

Butterscotch satin underlay

Whispering wind

Dressed in a delicate gown of chiffon and taffeta, Barbie captures the essence of a blowing breeze. This is from the Essence of Nature Series that is inspired by nature.

Windswept hair

White dove

Autumn glory

This doll in the Enchanted Seasons Collection is a romantic tribute to the beauty of the fall. The whole outfit shimmers with fall colors.

Water lily

This wonderful doll is the first in a series that celebrates the paintings of famous artists. In honor of the French artist Monet, Barbie doll's dress is decorated with water lilies made from layered gauze.

Fairy of the forest

Barbie is a lovely fairy in this shimmering, flowing gown from the Enchanted World of Fairies Series. Her delicate wings are dusted with golden glitter.

CAREER GIRL

FROM THE EARLY SIXTIES Barbie is seen as an independent career woman, but her job options are limited. With the Eighties comes the idea that women can do anything and Barbie takes on any career she wants.

BALLET COMPANY *Presents* NUTCRACKER SUITE
Sugar Plum Fairy..Barbie
Music........Tchaikowsky

Tutu

1991

Swan Lake Barbie
In this superb costume, Barbie dances the White Swan in the famous ballet by Tchaikovsky called "Swan Lake."

1961

Ballerina Barbie
Barbie doll's first ballet costume is for her role as the Sugar Plum Fairy in "The Nutcracker Suite."

1976

Ballerina Barbie
Graceful and charming, this Barbie can, with a child's help, do pirouettes, high kicks, and the splits.

Black practice leotard and pantyhose

BALLERINA

Many little girls want to be prima ballerinas when they grow up – here is Barbie to help fulfill all their dreams in these lovely costumes.

1998

Ballerina dreams
Everything about this blue-eyed Barbie gleams! She dances in a superb tutu with a shimmery bodice and a glittery overskirt.

Shimmery tulle tutu

1993

Ballerina Barbie
For the first time, My First Barbie wears molded on white pantyhose, panties, and pink ballet slippers.

Barbie dances on her toes

1961

Solo in the spotlight

Looking elegant in this long glittery knit dress, Barbie is a cool and sophisticated solo singer.

Pink 'n pretty Barbie
Here, Barbie is a glamorous pianist. She can captivate the audience with sweet ballads.

1987

Rocker Barbie

Here, Barbie wears silver stars and sings with her rock band The Rockers. Silver lamé and hot pink make this Eighties outfit truly glam rock.

This electric piano really works!

Fabric rose decoration

PERFORMER

Since the early Sixties, Barbie has been a star. Whenever Barbie puts on her fabulous costumes and makeup she takes center stage as a singer, rock group, or skating star. As the lights go up, she loves to go out and perform.

1998

Beyond pink

Barbie and her rock group Beyond Pink have a new hit single out – it's called "Think Pink."

1990

Ice Capades Barbie

Barbie is a graceful and glamorous skating star of the Ice Capades. Her costume glitters and floats as she skates.

Ice skate

1992

Rappin' rockin' Barbie

Barbie reflects the rap scene of the streets with her black and neon outfit and a boom box that plays a rap beat.

Barbie doll's boom box plays the beat

1961

Registered nurse

This Sixties nurse's uniform is designed along traditional lines with a heavy lined cape, which, today, nurses no longer wear.

Surgical gown and mask

1988

Doctor Barbie

Times have changed and women now find that they are positively encouraged to become doctors.

1973

Surgeon

After years of nursing, Barbie becomes a surgeon – showing girls that a career in medicine need not be restricted to nursing.

MEDICINE

Barbie doll's medical bag

Nursing has always been a popular career choice for women, but today women have branched out into all areas of medicine. Here, Barbie is dressed as a nurse, doctor, pet doctor, and dentist.

1997

Dentist

Dentist Barbie checks her young patient's teeth and shows her how to use a toothbrush correctly.

Magnifying mirror

1994

Pet doctor

Looking after dogs like this one is Pet Doctor Barbie doll's ideal job.

Dentist's chair

1994

Dr Barbie

In her job as a pediatrician, Barbie takes care of a newborn baby at the hospital.

Press the stethoscope against the baby's chest to hear her heart beat!

1965

1995

Teacher
This Nineties Barbie is now fully qualified to teach children, and she does it with style!

Student teacher
As a student teacher, Barbie is learning her job by giving a practice geography lesson.

Teaching globe

CARING CAREERS

In the caring professions – Barbie enjoys looking after people. Here, she is a teacher, a firefighter, and a police officer.

Protective helmet

1993

1994

Police officer
Barbie takes on the duties of a police woman with a smile. Police work is a tough job, but Barbie loves helping the community.

Firefighter
It is only fairly recently that women could become firefighters. Now they take on the same jobs as the men!

First aid kit box

Dalmatians are a traditional mascot

1966

Air stewardess

Barbie now works as an air stewardess for Pan Am airlines. She looks so efficient in this stylish twill suit.

1990

Air force

Captain Barbie is proud to be a pilot in the US Air Force where only the best are chosen to fly.

1993

Army

US Army medic Sergeant Barbie runs to help the wounded in the Gulf conflict. Barbie wears her 101st Airborne Division insignia with patriotic pride.

1961

Air stewardess

Barbie doll's new career as an air stewardess takes off with American Airlines.

1991

Navy

Petty Officer Barbie goes ashore for a well deserved furlough in her official new US naval uniform.

HIGHFLYERS

In the Sixties Barbie is a stewardess with the commercial airlines. Then her career takes off as Barbie becomes a pilot, an astronaut, and joins the armed forces.

U.S. AIR FORCE

ASTRONAUTS

Eighties space helmet

1965

Miss astronaut

Barbie wears her first astronaut outfit. It would be 20 years before a real woman would go into space!

1999

Pilot

Barbie reports for duty as a pilot for an airline company. It's a high profile career.

Up-to-date compact suitcase

Thigh-high boots

1986

Astronaut

Eighties Barbie is a glamorous astronaut in this glitter and lurex space uniform. It's an outfit that's based more on fun than on reality.

1994

Astronaut

Astronaut Barbie of the Nineties commemorates the earlier Apollo 11 moonwalk in her NASA helmet and spacesuit.

1960

1985

Day-to-night
This African-American Barbie is a hard-working business executive. Her vivid Eighties suit is ideal for the office. After work, the skirt can be turned inside out, making a glamorous evening outfit.

1978

Office girl
In the Seventies the hippy movement affects fashion and a more casual look is acceptable in the office.

POWER AND GLORY

In the Sixties women storm the business world. By the Nineties women have an impact in politics, and Barbie dresses for success to walk the corridors of power.

Busy gal
With her portfolio of designs, Barbie is a fashion designer. In the early Sixties matching hats are usually worn with suits to work.

1999

Working woman™
Dark colors are a must for suits in the Nineties. With her busy schedule Barbie is often on the go. There are always lots of calls to make on the mobile phone.

1991

Presidential candidate
When Barbie is on the campaign trail, by day she dresses in a wide-shouldered power suit – ideal for impressing her party delegates. At night she changes her outfit into this lovely gown for the Inaugural Ball!

Barbie checks her email on her laptop computer

Barbie doll's presidential button

DOLLS OF THE WORLD

IN 1980 A COLLECTOR'S SERIES called The Dolls of the World is introduced. These specially designed dolls are dressed in national costumes and have appropriate physical features. The dolls are fun to collect and also provide a useful starting point for exploring the culture of peoples around the world.

The Mountie's hat

Soft, fluffy faux fur

Inuit winter parka (coat)

NORTH AND CENTRAL AMERICA

Barbie can be seen here in costumes from across the vast continent of North America.

A military-style fitted jacket with silvery buttons

Riding jodhpurs (pants)

Headband design echoes the shape of a totem pole (below left)

ARCTIC BARBIE

Arctic Barbie (1997) is dressed in a winter outfit of the Inuit people. It keeps her warm in a snowy homeland. Her parka (coat) and hood are based on the traditional winter parka still worn today.

CANADIAN BARBIE

Here Canadian Barbie (1988) is dressed as a member of the Royal Canadian Mounted Police.

NORTHWEST COAST NATIVE AMERICAN BARBIE

This ceremonial dress of Northwest Coast Native American Barbie (2000) consists of a highly decorated blue dress topped by a fringed blanket or *Chil Kat*.

Traditional flower decoration

Totem pole from British Columbia, Canada

Traditional Mexican tile designs

Baby in papoose (sling)

NATIVE AMERICAN BARBIE

Although not part of The Dolls of the World series, this Native American Barbie (1997) celebrates the traditions of Native Americans. The buckskinlike fabric and fringe are elements of Native American style.

Brown and white ceremonial boots

MEXICAN BARBIE

Mexican Barbie (1996) wears a vivid outfit in the green and red colors which feature in the Mexican national flag. The bright patterns on the skirt are also seen in many Mexican pottery tile designs.

Straight brimmed black hat

A colorful sash

SOUTH AMERICA AND THE CARIBBEAN ISLANDS
Barbie wears the vibrant, colorful costumes of South America and the Caribbean.

CHILEAN BARBIE
Chilean Barbie (1998) wears a costume inspired by the *huasos* – Chilean cowboys.

Skirt split to show lacy panel

Black boots

Traditional serape

PERUVIAN BARBIE
Up in the high mountains of Peru, Peruvian Barbie (1999) wears a traditionally patterned skirt with a black underskirt. Her fringed *serape* (shawl) is useful for keeping out the cold when traveling and when carrying a young baby.

PUERTO RICAN BARBIE
Puerto Rican Barbie (1997) wears a dress made for special celebrations. The flower at her waist looks similar to the typical tropical flowers of this beautiful island.

Baby wears a hat decorated with a pompom

Flamboyant pink and silvery headdress

Stripes of woven pattern are typically Chilean

The bandana is tied in a knot on the head

JAMAICAN BARBIE
To keep cool in the tropical sun, Jamaican Barbie (1992) wears a long-sleeved, cotton dress. Her hair is tied back in a bandana – a typical headdress in this part of the world.

Patterned apron in quilted design

BRAZILIAN BARBIE
Carnivals are a colorful part of life in Brazil and often go on for many days. In this daring costume Brazilian Barbie (1990) can dance at the carnival.

Frilly ankle cuffs

DOLLS OF EUROPE

EUROPE IS A CONTINENT of contrasts – in culture, climate, and landscape. These differences are reflected in its wonderful mix of national costumes, from the cool blues of the Netherlands to the rich reds of Spain.

Traditional Scottish beret with pompom

SCOTTISH BARBIE
A red-haired Scottish Barbie (1991) wears a long skirt and sash in traditional Scots tartan. Her short jacket and lacy blouse are usually worn on ceremonial occasions.

Tartan colors and patterns vary depending on the clan (family) name

Delicate lace mob cap

Shamrock brooch

Shamrock

IRISH BARBIE
Red-haired Irish Barbie (1995) wears a taffeta dress in the vivid green of the Emerald Isle, as Ireland is often called, because of its lush green countryside. Her brooch features a shamrock, the Irish national symbol.

The elaborate dress hat is trimmed with tulle bows

ENGLISH BARBIE
Inspired by earlier times, when people wore such formal dress, this fair-haired English Barbie (1992) wears a fitted riding jacket over a full skirt.

Traditional Dutch lace cap

Embroidered apron

Her scarf is held by a lovely brooch

The mantilla (lace veil) is held in place by a peineta (comb)

SPANISH BARBIE
Red and yellow, which feature in the outfit of Spanish Barbie (1992), are popular colors in Spain – they are also the colors of the Spanish flag.

DUTCH BARBIE
This Dutch Barbie (1994) wears a simple but striking costume. Her skirt and bodice are in the sky blue of Delft pottery, for which the Netherlands is famous.

Nineteenth-century style buttoned boots

Laced black boots

FRENCH BARBIE
French Barbie (1997) wears the lace-frilled costume of a high-kicking can-can dancer. Black pantyhose and a large hat with feather wisps and flowers complete the picture.

Traditional
silver coin
necklace

Square-shaped hat

NORWEGIAN BARBIE
In this land of snow and midnight sun Norwegian Barbie (1996) wears a jumper called a *bunad* with an attractive floral design in a shade of blue that is typically Scandinavian.

RUSSIAN BARBIE
A vast country, Russia has many traditional costumes. The intricate cupola-shaped hat of the Russian Barbie costume (1997) is similar in shape to the domes of St. Basil's in Moscow and suggests eastern influences.

St. Basil's,
Moscow

Jumper

Big puffy
sleeves

Traditional
German braids

Fringed white
shawl

GERMAN BARBIE
From Bavaria – a region in Germany that is dotted with fairytale castles – this German Barbie (1995) is dressed in a traditional country-girl costume.

POLISH BARBIE
Polish Barbie (1998) is ready to dance the national dance, the polka, in her traditional peasant dress. Her decorated black vest and colorful crown of flowers with ribbons are features of Polish costumes.

Ribbons are
a traditional
headdress

Hooped
earrings

ITALIAN BARBIE
Raven-haired Italian Barbie (1993) wears a costume in Neapolitan style with ribbons decorating the jacket and apron. Her full taffeta skirt is ideal for dancing the national dance, called the tarantella.

Fine lace
apron

Embroidered
lapels

AUSTRIAN BARBIE
Austrian Barbie (1999) wears a delicate floral skirt with ribbon and lace trims. The flowers on her skirt and lapels are based on the mass of alpine flowers that cover the mountains in spring.

A red waist
sash matches
her red
pantyhose

Wild alpine
flower

Long black
boots

CZECHOSLOVAKIAN BARBIE
Red, black, and yellow are the main colors worn by Czechoslovakian Barbie (1991) in traditional folk costume. Her blouse is trimmed with eyelet lace.

AFRICA, ASIA, AND AUSTRALASIA

HAVE LOTS OF FUN exploring the diverse costumes of three continents with Barbie. You can see colorful and highly patterned designs of costumes from Africa, a fabulous Indian sari, a Japanese kimono, and a sarong from East Asia, as well as typical outfits from Australia and the Pacific region.

Indian sari fabric

Coin necklace

INDIAN BARBIE

Here Indian Barbie (1996) wears a traditional sari. This is a long piece of fabric which is wrapped around the body and draped over one shoulder. It is usually worn with a short bodice underneath. Red is often worn by brides as a symbol of good luck.

MOROCCAN BARBIE

Moroccan Barbie (1999) wears a splendid scarlet and gold costume. In the Middle East, coins are often worn as jewelry. The coin circlet around the forehead and her necklace are traditional signs of wealth.

NIGERIAN BARBIE

This Nigerian Barbie (1990) wears a two-piece costume with intricately patterned fabric that is typical of the region.

Head scarf

Bead necklaces show wealth and status

The loose and simple shape is ideal for the hot African climate

GHANAIAN BARBIE

Ghanaian Barbie (1996) wears the bright colors and geometric patterns of this region. The head scarf shows her social position — the higher it is, the more important she is.

Original Maasai necklace

KENYAN BARBIE

Layers of colorful necklaces and a vivid cloak tied by a large knot give this Kenyan Barbie (1994) a traditional Maasai look. After marriage, Maasai girls often wear more necklaces to indicate their status.

CHINESE BARBIE

Chinese Barbie (1994) is wearing a long silk *cheongsam* with slits at the side, under a jacket with Mandarin-style sleeves. Her costume has a chrysanthemum pattern; these flowers are symbols of long life in China.

Chrysanthemum flowers

Temple-shaped headdress

Cheongsam dress

Korean hat

KOREAN BARBIE

Korean Barbie (1988) wears a costume in the traditional Korean style – a high-waisted dress in brilliant colors.

JAPANESE BARBIE

This Japanese Barbie (1996) wears a ceremonial kimono tied at the waist with a wide gold *obi* (belt). She also wears traditional Japanese *zori* (slippers) over *tabi* – special white socks with toes.

Obi (belt)

Zori (slippers)

A typical temple in Thailand

Bushman's hat

AUSTRALIAN BARBIE

Australian Barbie (1993) is ready to tackle anything – from horseback riding to exploring – in this practical jacket and skirt. Her *akubra* (bushman's) hat keeps off the hot sun.

Lace trim

THAI BARBIE

Thai Barbie (1998) wears a fabulous dance costume from Thailand. Her headdress resembles the golden temples that are a feature of the Thai countryside.

Thai dancers are always barefoot

Fabric rose

MALAYSIAN BARBIE

Malaysian Barbie (1991) looks gorgeous in an elegant taffeta jacket over a sarong-style dress. Her golden necklace is a traditional decoration.

POLYNESIAN BARBIE

The swinging grass-style skirt and *lei* (garland) of flowers are traditional elements of the costume of Polynesian Barbie (1996). These flowers are typical in the Pacific islands.

SPORTS DOLLS

NOTHING COULD BE FINER than physical activities in the great outdoors. Summer or winter, Barbie and Ken enjoy any sport. They find it makes them feel healthy and happy, too.

SUMMER FUN

When summer arrives Barbie and Ken can spend lots of time having fun outdoors. They enjoy windsurfing, sailing, and swimming.

1981

Roller skating

More fun than jogging but just as energetic, in the Eighties going skating with Ken is one of Barbie doll's favorite outdoor activities.

Barbie and Ken wear matching outfits

Roller skate

1975

Hawaiian Barbie

The art of surfboarding is to skim along the surface of the waves using the wind. Keeping upright on the board is hard work – no wonder Barbie needs a rest!

1992

Rollerblade Barbie

These in-line skates are the latest way to skate. It's fun, but tough to get it right. Sidewalks are hard so Barbie wears knee and wrist guards to avoid getting scrapes and sprains.

Video camera

Protective knee pads

In-line skates that flicker and flash as they roll!

Flippers

Keiko the baby whale

1999

Ocean magic Barbie

Barbie swims with her friend Keiko. Her wetsuit disappears when she's in warm water. Now that is amazing!

WINTER SPORTS

When it's snowy Barbie and Ken like to ski, skate, or go sledding with their friends. It's great fun! Barbie always remembers to dress warmly.

Sun glasses are essential

Removable imitation fur collar

Wooly hat

1963

Ski queen Barbie
Barbie and Ski Champion Alan take to the slopes for the first time in 1963. Their ski outfits, ski bindings, and wooden poles look old-fashioned now.

Simple bindings

1965

Skater's waltz
Gliding beautifully over the ice takes skill and lots of practice. This cute outfit is perfect for showing off skating technique.

Earmuffs keep out the cold

1999

Winter fun
Sledding is more a pastime than a sport for Barbie, but there is nothing nicer when it's snowy out.

1992

Skiing
Ski Fun Barbie doll's Nineties ski outfit is neon bright. Barbie and Ken also wear modern ski boots and have high-tech ski poles.

Protective headgear

Ski pass

1992

Snowboarding
Ski Fun Ken is going snowboarding. The newest sport for energetic people, this requires good balance, strength, and nerve to fly down the slopes on one large board.

Warm snow boots

KEEPING FIT IS FUN!

Barbie makes the most of her leisure time playing tennis, walking, horseback riding, and working out. These activities are all great fun and help keep Barbie trim and shapely all year round.

Cotton tennis sweater

Tennis anyone?

Barbie takes up tennis in the early Sixties. It's a great sport for keeping in shape and meeting new friends.

1973

Hiker Barbie

When Barbie goes walking or hiking she takes a backpack with supplies of water and energy snacks.

Sun visor

1974

Two for tennis?

Barbie and Ken often play tennis together in doubles matches. They are both dressed in the correct outfits for top level tennis.

1984

Great shape Barbie

Barbie goes to aerobics classes every week to keep herself fit and supple. Her leotard and legwarmers are the latest exercise gear.

Legwarmers

Sports bag

1994

Gymnast Barbie

Barbie does stretching exercises and works out at the gym to increase her strength and stamina.

1998

Horse Riding Barbie

Barbie loves to ride in equestrian events. Here, Barbie doll's riding outfit is a velveteen jacket, a hard riding hat, and long black boots.

OLYMPIC COMPETITOR

It takes a lot of practice and dedication to get on the team for the Olympic Games. Barbie is a trained sportswoman in many events and has won many gold medals for her country.

1975

1975

Olympic skier
Ken enters the cross-country skiing event in the 1976 Innsbruck Winter Olympics.

1975

Olympic gymnast PJ
Barbie doll's friend PJ performs her winning routine on the balance beam in the 1976 Montreal Summer Olympics.

Balance beam

Olympic gold medal

Olympic skater
Barbie skates for her country and wins a gold medal in the 1976 Innsbruck Winter Olympics cross-country event.

2000

Protective helmet

Paralympic Becky
Here, Barbie doll's friend Becky is an eager member of the paralympic team competing in the wheelchair events in Sydney, Australia.

Gloves protect the hands

1996

Olympic gymnast
Barbie wins a medal in the Atlanta Olympic Games when she competes as a gymnast.

2000

Swimming champion
Here Barbie is a winning member of the US swimming team in the first Olympic Games of the new millennium in Sydney, Australia.

ON THE CATWALK

BARBIE HAS ALWAYS been at the forefront of fashion. In the early Nineties, this is celebrated with the launch of Mattel's Classique Collection, a series of stunning dolls created by Mattel's own fashion designers. Today, Barbie also appears in fabulous costumes designed by couturiers of international fame.

Benefit ball Barbie

Carol Spencer, legendary Barbie doll designer, created this gorgeous ball gown to launch the Classique Collection in 1992. Her Benefit Ball Barbie is the first redhead to be released in nearly 20 years.

Sparkling blue pendant

A wondrous boa wraps around her shoulders and ends in a majestic, sweeping flounce

Shimmering gold lamé

Blue metallic jacquard fabric

Flowing silky crepe skirt with sparkling chiffon panels

Hair styled in an elegant upward swirl

Jewel encrusted headband

Starlight dance

Created by Mattel designer Cynthia Young, this beautiful gown is made of silky crepe with delicate chiffon panels. Like other Classique Collection dolls, it comes with a biography of the designer.

Givenchy

Barbie looks back to the past in this classic reproduction of a 1956 gown by Givenchy, a designer who was renowned for his sophisticated ballgowns.

Glamorous Fifties hairstyle

Velvet straps

Faux fur stole with moiré lining

Sparkling crystal rhinestones decorate the sheer fitted bodice

Long, slim fitting gown in moiré taffeta

Fishtail skirt

**Short and stylish
sideswept cut**

Head turner
The vibrant dress features a stunning low back, lined with fuchsia and decorated with an oversized cabbage rose.

Fuchsia tulle underskirt for added fullness

Tangerine twist
Created by Mattel designer Kitty Black Perkins, this doll is in the Fashion Savvy Collection, the only series to consist entirely of African-American Barbie dolls. These glamorous fashions reflect the style of contemporary African-American women.

Leopard print hat with feathers

Leather-look gloves and handbag

Celebrity gala
This stunning, empire-line gown reflects the dramatic flair of its designer, Bill Blass, known for his fabulous evening dresses designed for celebrities.

Striking oversized bow in black and white stripes

Satiny suit

Long, dramatic train

Stunning hairstyle piled high on head

Faux fur collar decorated with diamond stud brooch

Metallic fabric cape lined in luscious lime

Faux fur cuffs

Chocolate brown, velvety dress with split skirt

Evening illusion
This dream of a dress by top couturier designer Nolan Miller is of blue satin-like fabric overlaid with black lace.

Champagne colored bodice overlaid with lace

In the limelight
Created by talented designer Bryon Lars, this bold and dynamic Barbie is part of the Runway Collection, which celebrates contemporary fashions.

Elegant hairstyle

Golden drop earrings

Luxurious faux fur stole

Long, elegant train with intricate beading and scalloped trim

107

BOB MACKIE

Fashion costume designer for the stage, screen, and television, Bob Mackie brings his own inspired, imaginative ideas to the world of the Barbie doll. These wonderful creations reflect Mackie's love of fantasy and grandeur, and display his meticulous attention to detail.

Hair is coiled and arranged in a high ponytail

Amazing raised collar with leaf shapes

High ponytail tied with golden hooped headpiece

Gold Barbie
Released in 1990, this glamorous creation was the first to appear in the Bob Mackie series and is today one of the most sought-after by collectors.

Original sketch

Crossover bodice

Neptune fantasy
Barbie rises from the sea in 1992 in this extraordinary creation.

Skirt made up of thousands of golden sequins

Sequin-covered dress

Velvet cloak of sea green

Long feather boa

Fantastic fan
decorated with a
Chinese dragon

Delicate sheer
netting covered
with beading

Golden fan

Long wrap
skirt covered
in bugle beads

Original
sketch

Fantasy goddess of Asia

This Asian Barbie
is the first to appear
in Bob Mackie's
International Beauty
Collection, created to
celebrate worldwide
beauty. The gown is
influenced by the
strong colors and
shapes of the East.

Headpiece
made of
orange and
red feathers

Golden
neckpiece
with colorful
beadwork

Beaded
arm bands

Fantasy goddess of Africa

Mackie takes
traditional African
dress and patterning
and adds his own
personal touch to
create this
wonderful African
fantasy doll.

Gown is richly
embroidered and
heavily beaded

Original
sketch

STARSTRUCK

FROM THE EARLY NINETIES onward, Barbie shows true star quality. Dressed in exquisite replica costumes of Hollywood legends of the silver screen, Barbie is a show stopper.

MARILYN MONROE

Rhinestone bracelet

Long silk gloves

Rhinestone necklace and earrings

SCARLETT O'HARA

Red feather trim

Stunning off-the-shoulder dress in pink satin

Southern belle
In 1994, Barbie steps out as the willful beauty Scarlett O'Hara, from the Turner Classics film *Gone With the Wind*, which starred Vivien Leigh.

Stunning red velvet gown

Oversized bow with contrasting taffeta lining

Gentlemen prefer blondes
Barbie poses as Marilyn Monroe in the 1953 movie *Gentlemen Prefer Blondes*. She wears a replica of the pink satin dress worn by Marilyn as she sang "Diamonds are a Girl's Best Friend."

Feather decoration

TRUE TREASURES

These fabulous creations from the Timeless Treasures series celebrate the talents of two legendary movie stars. These dolls are different from the Hollywood Barbie dolls (*see left*) because they have special face sculpts that are true to the features of the actresses.

Golden goddess
This replica doll pays tribute to the beautiful and glamorous Elizabeth Taylor in her role as Cleopatra in the epic 1963 movie of the same name.

ELIZABETH TAYLOR

Heavy kohl eyeliner and glitter eyeshadow

The clever sculpting captures the stunning beauty of Elizabeth Taylor

Golden gown with dramatic "feather" cloak

Rhinestone tiara

AUDREY HEPBURN

Elegant upswept hairstyle

Face sculpting captures the gamine beauty of Audrey Hepburn

Sophisticated lady
This stunning doll has all the grace and elegance of Audrey Hepburn in her role as Holly Golightly in the 1961 movie, *Breakfast at Tiffany's.*

Triple-strand faux pearl necklace

Black opera gloves

Long, sleeveless gown

White stole

STAGE AND SCREEN

BARBIE HAS LOTS OF FUN pretending to be a host of characters on the stage, screen, and television. Whether performing a pirouette, quoting lines of Shakespeare, or being beamed up to the Starship *Enterprise*, Barbie is always the star of the show!

Forever in love

Barbie and Ken appear as star-crossed lovers Romeo and Juliet, the first in the Together Forever Collection, a series of dolls inspired by the romance of legendary couples. The costumes brilliantly recreate the richness of 16th century fashions.

Off to see the wizard!

In 1995, Barbie takes a trip along the Yellow Brick Road as Dorothy in the Turner Classics film *The Wizard of Oz*, starring Judy Garland. Ken joins her a year later as Scarecrow, Tin Man, and Cowardly Lion.

Braided hair

Crisp white blouse with puffy sleeves

Dorothy's dog Toto

Blue gingham jumper

Magical Ruby Slippers

Sugar plum fairy

Barbie dances *en pointe* as the Sugar Plum Fairy in Tchaikovsky's ballet, "The Nutcracker Suite." This is the first in the Classic Ballet Series, featuring dolls dressed in costumes from the world's best-loved ballets.

Ivory bodice trimmed with ribbons

Skirt made of shimmering layers of light pink tulle

Ken as Tin Man from The Wizard of Oz. *He has a poseable body and comes with an oil can, ax, and a heart-shaped clock, just like in the movie!*

Rosie O'Donnell

This is a 1999 "Friend of Barbie" who looks just like her television celebrity namesake. Rosie requested that part of the proceeds from this doll's sales go to her charity, The For All Kids Foundation®.

Stylish red pantsuit

Badge of Courage

Barbie poses as an Engineering Officer in her authentic red uniform with black trim

As Commanding Officer, Ken wears a gold jersey and insignia

Star Trek Insignia

Phaser

Tricorder

Star trek

Barbie and Ken boldly go where no man has gone before in this 30th anniversary tribute to the Sixties *Star Trek* television series. The dolls appear in a fun, commemorative package with pictures of Captain Kirk and First Officer Spock. This giftset belongs to the Barbie Loves Pop Culture series.

Courtesy of Paramount Pictures. *Star Trek* © 2000 by Paramount Pictures. All rights reserved.

Ken as Cowardly Lion in a fleecy lion suit just like in the movie, The Wizard of Oz.

THE BARBIE DYNASTY

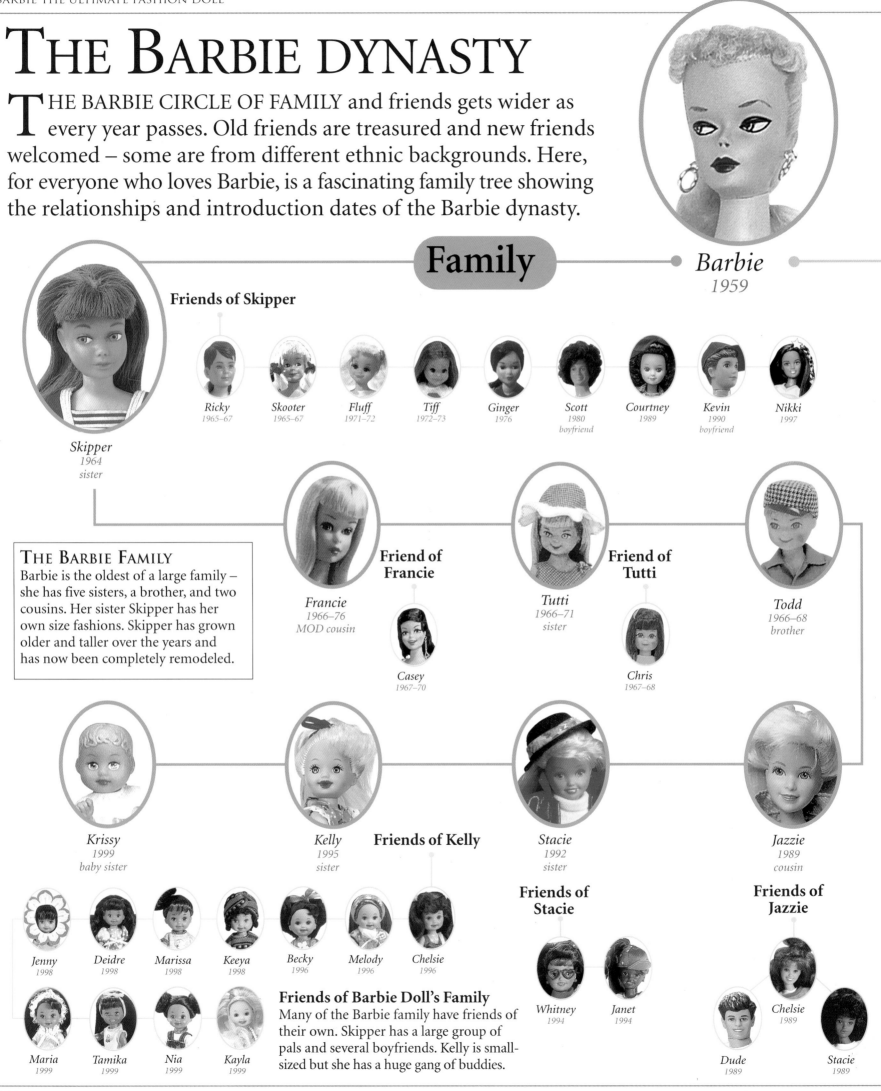

THE BARBIE CIRCLE OF FAMILY and friends gets wider as every year passes. Old friends are treasured and new friends welcomed – some are from different ethnic backgrounds. Here, for everyone who loves Barbie, is a fascinating family tree showing the relationships and introduction dates of the Barbie dynasty.

Family

Barbie
1959

Friends of Skipper

Ricky
1965–67

Skooter
1965–67

Fluff
1971–72

Tiff
1972–73

Ginger
1976

Scott
1980
boyfriend

Courtney
1989

Kevin
1990
boyfriend

Nikki
1997

Skipper
1964
sister

THE BARBIE FAMILY
Barbie is the oldest of a large family – she has five sisters, a brother, and two cousins. Her sister Skipper has her own size fashions. Skipper has grown older and taller over the years and has now been completely remodeled.

Friend of Francie

Francie
1966–76
MOD cousin

Casey
1967–70

Friend of Tutti

Tutti
1966–71
sister

Chris
1967–68

Todd
1966–68
brother

Krissy
1999
baby sister

Kelly
1995
sister

Friends of Kelly

Stacie
1992
sister

Jazzie
1989
cousin

Jenny
1998

Deidre
1998

Marissa
1998

Keeya
1998

Becky
1996

Melody
1996

Chelsie
1996

Friends of Stacie

Friends of Jazzie

Maria
1999

Tamika
1999

Nia
1999

Kayla
1999

Friends of Barbie Doll's Family
Many of the Barbie family have friends of their own. Skipper has a large group of pals and several boyfriends. Kelly is small-sized but she has a huge gang of buddies.

Whitney
1994

Janet
1994

Dude
1989

Chelsie
1989

Stacie
1989

FRIENDS

Barbie doll's first friends are Ken, her boyfriend, and Midge, her best friend. Then Christie, an African-American friend is introduced. As time goes on, new friends arrive who reflect the interests of girls in each decade. In 1997, Barbie has a differently-abled friend, called Becky.

Friends and Family of Ken

Allan (later Alan)
1964–65, 1991
boyfriend, then
husband of Midge

Brad
1970
friend of Ken

Curtis
1975
boyfriend of Cara

Todd
1983
fiancé of Tracy

Derek
1986
friend of Ken

Steven
1988
Christie doll's boyfriend

Tommy
1997
brother

Friends

Ken
1961
boyfriend of Barbie

Midge
1963
best friend

Christie
1968

Stacey
1968–70

PJ
1969

Diva
1986

Dana
1986

Tracy
1983

Cara
1975–78

Kelley
1973–76

Steffie
1972–73

Jamie
1970–72

Dee Dee
1986

Whitney
1987

Miko
1987

Bopsy
1988

Belinda
1988

Becky
1988

Teresa
1988

Shani
1994

Tara Lynn
1993

Nia
1990

Kira
1990

Devon
1989

Nikki
1989

Kayla
1989

Becky
1997

Ana
1999

Chelsie
1999

Lara
1999

Nichelle
1999

Tori
1999

The Future
The world of Barbie doll will keep expanding in 2000 and beyond!

FRIENDS AND FAMILY

B ARBIE IS A SUCCESSFUL DOLL – but she needs a life too! She has a boyfriend, a sister called Skipper and, as time goes on, cousins, lots of friends, and new young members who join an ever-increasing family circle.

KEN

Ken is introduced as Barbie doll's boyfriend in 1961 and has stayed by her side ever since. Starting out with nine outfits, a skinny frame and a fuzzy crewcut, Ken has changed with the times, but he is still a handsome hunk of a guy.

1991

Hawaiian fun Ken
Here's Ken on vacation with two-tone blonde hair and a tanned body.

Painted hair

Flocked hair which rubs off when wet

1961

Busy Ken
Now Ken doll's face is wider, his body and limbs are chunkier, and he has a nice smile too.

1972

1981

Malibu Ken
The Eighties see the arrival of the first African-American Ken with a big Afro hairstyle.

Shave 'n style Ken
With his stylish hairstyle, goatee beard, and relaxed smile, Ken looks very hip in the late Nineties.

Campus hero
Ken goes to college and Barbie is his date at football games.

Meet Ken doll's friends

Ken
Here is Ken doll's first outfit – a red swimsuit and sandals.

Free moving Curtis
Ken doll's sporty buddy Curtis arrives in 1974. A lever allows him to move easily.

1990

Hawaiian fun Steven
Steven joins Ken and Barbie on their Hawaiian fun vacation.

1991

Wedding day Alan
This is Ken doll's pal Alan (formerly called Allan) on his wedding day to Midge, Barbie doll's friend, in 1991.

SKIPPER

Barbie has a new sister in 1964 called Skipper. In the early days, she's much shorter than Barbie – just 9¼ in (23.5 cm) tall – and has long straight red hair that can be brushed. She has her own wardrobe too.

1973

1980

1991

Quick curl Skipper
Blonde Skipper still looks like a young girl here in her gingham granny frock.

Skipper
Little sister Skipper wears a cute swimsuit on her arrival in 1964.

Ricky
A freckle-faced kid with red hair and blue eyes, Ricky is Skipper doll's friend from 1965 to 1967.

Super teen Skipper
Skipper is growing up fast and has a new boyfriend called Scott.

Coolest kids
Teenager Skipper and her boyfriend Kevin are the coolest kids on the block.

Meet Barbie doll's family

Babysitter Skipper
Skipper is always being asked to babysit! Here, she has two to look after. She looks quite grown-up now.

1999

Bowling party Stacie
Barbie doll's small sister Stacie arrives in 1992. Here she is going bowling.

Little friends

Skooter is Skipper doll's friend from 1965 to 1967. She is cute, with freckles and pigtails. Here, she holds the hand of Tutti – a little sister of Barbie.

Francie

Barbie doll's cousin Francie is a big part of her life from 1966 to 1976. She has a "Mod" wardrobe all her own.

1966

Todd
Brother of Barbie, Todd is ring bearer at the wedding of Barbie doll's friends Midge and Alan.

1991

Krissy
Barbie doll's baby sister Krissy arrives in 1999.

Kelly
Barbie doll's baby sister Kelly plays with her friend Tommy, little brother of Ken.

Hawaiian fun Jazzie

In 1989 Barbie has a new cousin called Jazzie.

1990

1999

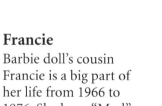

BARBIE DOLL'S FRIENDS

Over the years Barbie makes many friends. Her first and best friend is Midge who appears in 1963. From then on, Barbie becomes ever more popular as she surrounds herself with a growing band of fun-loving friends.

At the beach
Surf's up for Malibu Skipper, Christie, Barbie, and Ken, seen here on a California beach in 1978.

1978

Teresa
Teresa is Barbie doll's first Hispanic friend who is introduced in 1988. After a new face sculpt in 1991, this is how Teresa looks today.

Stacey

This is Barbie doll's British pal from 1968 to 1970. This doll also comes with red hair.

1968

PJ
In 1969 Barbie doll's fun new friend called PJ comes on the scene.

1969

Talking Christie
Barbie doll's first African-American friend arrives in 1968. She can talk, too.

1968

Meet Barbie doll's friends

Midge
Freckle-faced Midge, Barbie doll's best friend, is introduced in 1963. The same size as Barbie, Midge can wear all of Barbie doll's outfits.

Jamie
Jamie is Barbie doll's friend from 1970 to 1972.

Wedding Day Midge

After a long absence, Midge reappears in 1988. In 1991 she marries her childhood sweetheart Alan (formerly spelt Allan), in a romantic white wedding. Her best friend Barbie is maid of honor.

1988

Steffie
In 1972 Barbie meets a new pal called Steffie.

1972

1973

Quick Curl Kelley
Kelley is a friend who is around for a short while from 1973 to 1976.

1983

Wedding Day
Barbie doll's best friend Tracy and Ken doll's friend Todd are pictured here on their wedding day.

1990

All-American Kira
Barbie doll's fun Asian friend Kira arrives in 1990. Just look at those earrings!

All three friends wear the star-spangled denim look

Friends forever
All-American Christie, Ken, and Barbie are having a great day out together.

Ken wears big baggy jeans – the latest fashion

1991

Shani
Barbie doll's friend Shani arrives in 1991. Here in 1994, she is a children's doctor.

1994

Share a smile Becky
Becky is one of Barbie doll's latest friends and is introduced in 1997. She is a new role model for children of differing abilities.

BARBIE PETS

Barbie is a true animal lover. Over the years she has collected more than 35 pets including dogs, cats, horses, and a giraffe. Here are a few of her favorites.

Beauty and the beasts
Here, Barbie doll's gorgeous 1982 Afghan hound called Beauty plays with her cute puppies.

Dog 'n duds
The first pet that Barbie owns in 1964 is this tiny miniature poodle.

Pure breed
Lucky Barbie gets this Arabian horse in 1988. He is called Blinking Beauty.

Pony pals
This is Barbie and her new All-American horse in 1991. The horse is an Arabian breed.

Tiffy
Tag Along Tiffy is on wheels and has fashion finesse in 1993.

Sachi
This is just the coolest dog dude isn't it? He is from 1992.

Puppy ruff
This Scottish Terrier barks when petted. He arrives in 1994.

CHANGING FACE

WHEN THE BARBIE DOLL first appeared in 1959, she was marketed as a "teenage fashion model," and her slim body and well-groomed appearance reflected this. Over the years Barbie has changed in many ways, but it is her face that has altered the most. Today's wide eyes and smile are a far cry from the sophisticated look of 1959 with her pursed lips and flirtatious sideways glance.

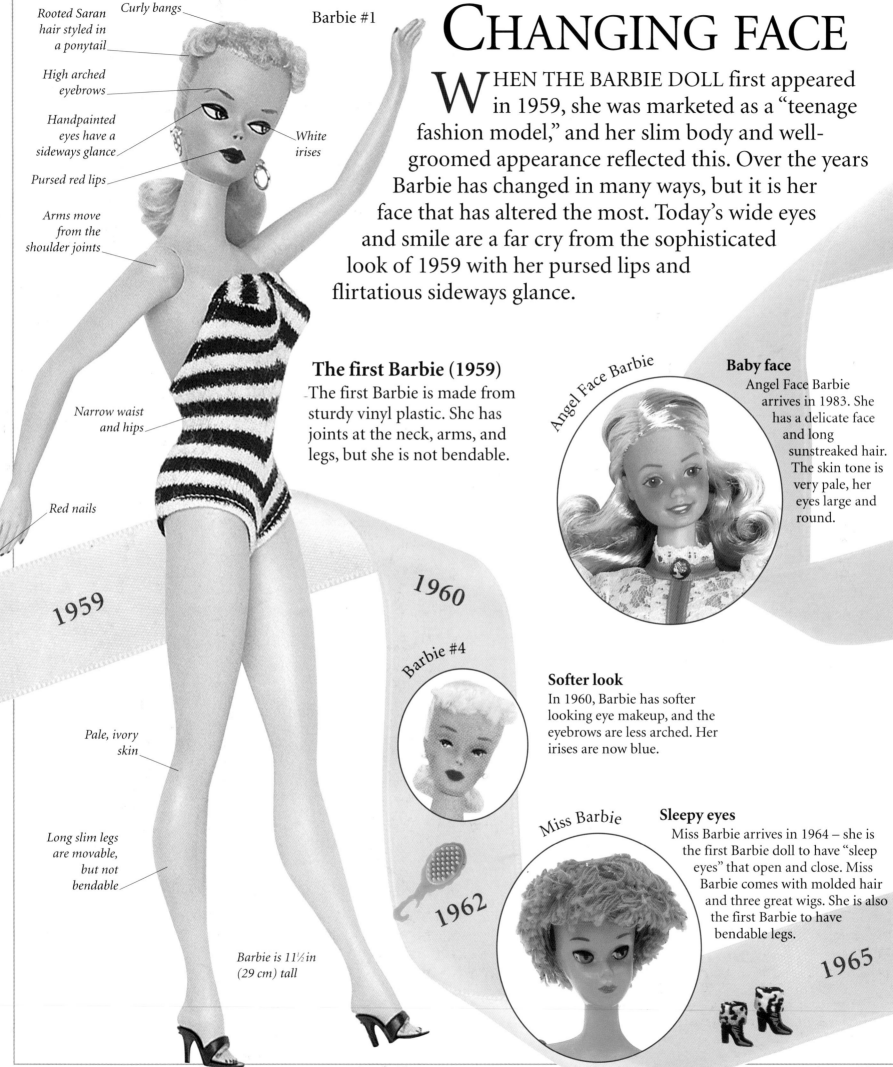

Rooted Saran hair styled in a ponytail

Curly bangs

Barbie #1

High arched eyebrows

Handpainted eyes have a sideways glance

White irises

Pursed red lips

Arms move from the shoulder joints

Narrow waist and hips

Red nails

Pale, ivory skin

Long slim legs are movable, but not bendable

Barbie is 11½ in (29 cm) tall

1959

1960

Barbie #4

1962

The first Barbie (1959)
The first Barbie is made from sturdy vinyl plastic. She has joints at the neck, arms, and legs, but she is not bendable.

Angel Face Barbie

Baby face
Angel Face Barbie arrives in 1983. She has a delicate face and long sunstreaked hair. The skin tone is very pale, her eyes large and round.

Softer look
In 1960, Barbie has softer looking eye makeup, and the eyebrows are less arched. Her irises are now blue.

Miss Barbie

Sleepy eyes
Miss Barbie arrives in 1964 – she is the first Barbie doll to have "sleep eyes" that open and close. Miss Barbie comes with molded hair and three great wigs. She is also the first Barbie to have bendable legs.

1965

Bath Boutique Barbie

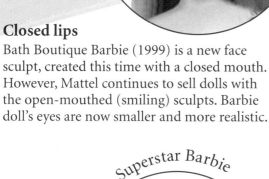

2000

1999

Closed lips

Bath Boutique Barbie (1999) is a new face sculpt, created this time with a closed mouth. However, Mattel continues to sell dolls with the open-mouthed (smiling) sculpts. Barbie doll's eyes are now smaller and more realistic.

Natural looking makeup

Wide eyes looking straight ahead

Jewel Girl Barbie

Smiling lips

Barbie today

Barbie today can have a more natural, supple body. The new model launched in 2000 has a soft tummy area, a flexible waist, and a smaller upper body. She even has a belly button!

"LA tan" skin tone

Superstar Barbie

The glam look

The third major face change for the Barbie doll, Superstar Barbie (1977) has a bigger smile and fuller hair – in keeping with the glamorous style of the Seventies. At first, Mattel only produce blonde Barbie dolls with this sculpt.

1976

Long, loose hair can be styled in a variety of ways

Twist 'N Turn Barbie

1970

Malibu Barbie

A fresh look

In response to comments that the original Barbie looked too sophisticated and old to be a "teenage fashion model," Twist 'N Turn Barbie (1967) arrives. She has a new face mold with a younger look. She has lighter makeup, rooted eyelashes, and straight shiny hair.

The natural look

The first Malibu Barbie (1972) uses the Stacey head mold and personifies the California look – suntanned, makeup free, with long, straight hair.

PACKING UP

THE CARRYING CASE is an important status symbol for any self-respecting Barbie owner. Not only is it a handy unit in which to keep all Barbie doll's clothes and accessories, but it is also the ideal way to take everything to a friend's home for fun playtime and fashion comparisons.

EARLY PACKAGING

The first box is illustrated with the 21 fashions available in the stores. For wholesale trade buyers, a special pink box with silhouettes is produced. From the mid-Sixties, the boxes are enlivened with a main photographic image. Each box makes a handy individual carrying case.

Trade box 1959

Barbie 1959

Barbie doll case 1961

Barbie doll case 1963

Barbie doll case 1961

Clothes and things

No detail is overlooked, whether it is a teacher's globe or Skipper doll's gramophone. Accessories are displayed enticingly on a cardboard backdrop.

Ken doll case 1962

Barbie and Midge case 1963

Chic cases

These carrying cases sport images of Barbie, Francie, Midge, or Ken in the latest fashions. Inside there is space for the doll, accessories, and a clothes rail on which the clothes can hang.

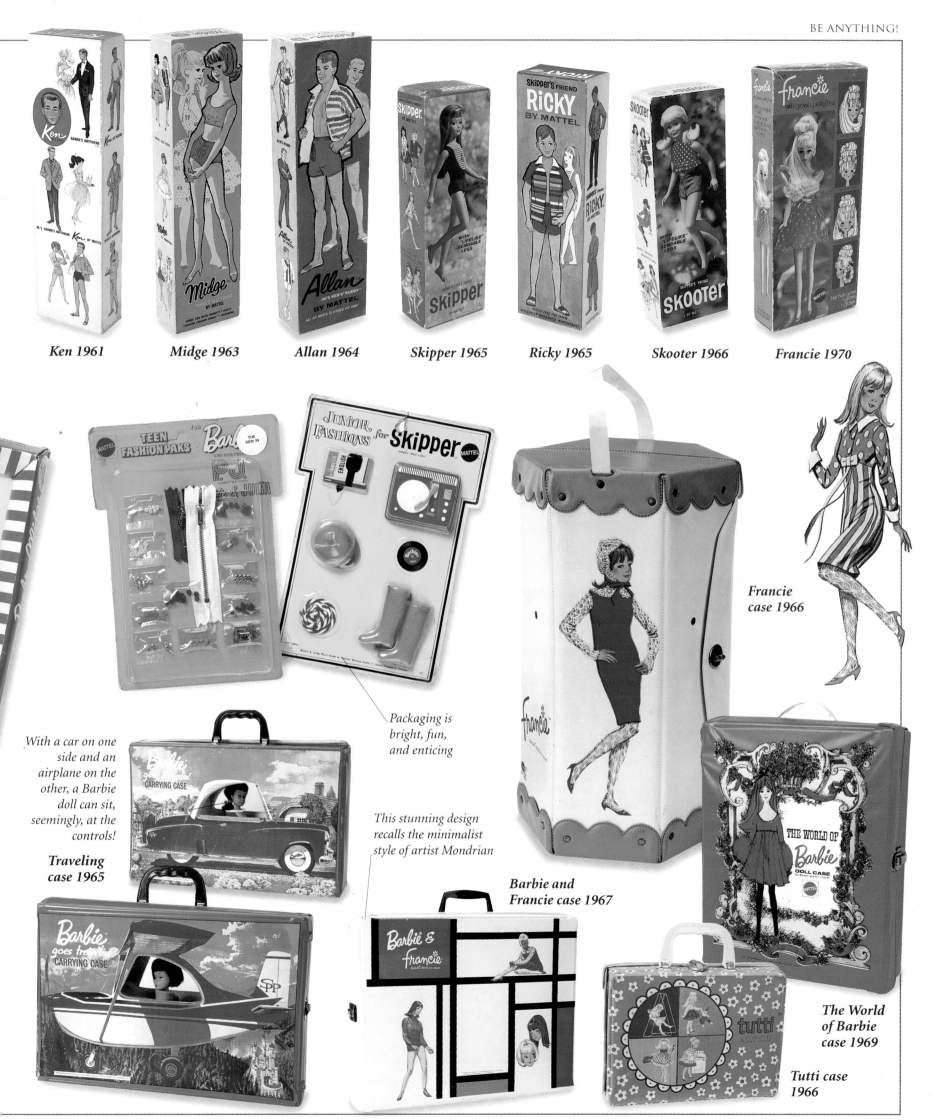

Ken 1961

Midge 1963

Allan 1964

Skipper 1965

Ricky 1965

Skooter 1966

Francie 1970

Packaging is bright, fun, and enticing

Francie case 1966

With a car on one side and an airplane on the other, a Barbie doll can sit, seemingly, at the controls!

Traveling case 1965

This stunning design recalls the minimalist style of artist Mondrian

Barbie and Francie case 1967

The World of Barbie case 1969

Tutti case 1966

CATALOG OF DOLLS AND OUTFITS

NB The dolls and accessories are listed here with their toy years, not their original copyright, or box, years. Because of this, there may be some discrepancies with the dates given in the text of the book. Names of dolls and accessories shown in quotes are descriptive names only, not Mattel names. All product numbers listed are US numbers.

pp. 12–13
Barbie Ponytail #1, 1959, #850, p. 12
Resort Set, 1959, #963, p. 12
Evening Splendor, 1959, #961, p. 12
Suburban Shopper, 1959, #969, p. 12
Picnic Set, 1959, #967, p. 12
Friday Nite Date, 1960, #979, p. 12
Solo in the Spotlight, 1960, #982, p. 12
Busy Gal, 1960, #981, p. 12
Enchanted Evening, 1960, #983, p. 13
    Ken doll, 1961, #750, p. 13
        Registered Nurse, 1961, #991, p. 13
        Open Road, 1961, #985, p. 13
        Austin Healey car, 1962, made by Irwin Corp. for Mattel, p.13
        Dreamboat Ken, 1961, # 785, p. 13
    Ballerina, 1961, #989, p. 13
Bubblecut Barbie, 1961, #850, p. 13
Garden Party, 1962, #931, p. 13

pp. 14–15
Sweater Girl, 1959, #976, p. 14
Tennis Anyone?, 1962, #941, p. 14
Red Flare, 1962, #939, p. 14
Dreamboat, 1961, #785, p. 14
Graduation, 1963, #945, p. 14
Career Girl, 1963, #954, p. 14
Bride's Dream, 1963, #947, and Tuxedo, 1961, #787, p. 14
Barbie Babysits, 1963, #953, p. 14
Fashion Queen, 1963, #870, p. 14
Midge doll, 1963, #860, p.15
Icebreaker, 1962, #942, p. 15
Theater Date, 1963, #959, p. 15
Sophisticated Lady, 1963, #993, p. 15
Barbie Swirl ponytail, 1964, #850, p. 15
Raincoat, 1963, #949, p. 15
Black Magic, 1964, #1609, p. 15
Allan doll, 1964, #1000, p. 15
Skipper doll, 1964, #0950, p. 15
Miss Barbie, 1964, #1060, p. 15

pp. 16–17
It's Cold Outside, 1964, #819, p. 16
Midge Bendable Leg, 1965, #1080, p. 16
Midnight Blue, 1965, #1617, p. 16
American Girl Barbie, 1965, #1070, p. 16
Magnificence, 1965, #1646, p. 16
Gold 'N Glamor, 1965, #1647, p. 16
Ricky doll, 1965, #1090, p. 16
    Skooter Bendable Leg, 1966, #1120, p. 16
        Fashion Luncheon, 1966, #1656, p. 17
    Sunday Visit, 1966, #1675, p. 17
    Evening Gala, 1966, #1660, p. 17
Club Meeting, 1966, #1672, p. 17
Casey doll, 1967, #1180, Style

Setters, 1966, #1268, p. 17
Twiggy doll, 1967, #1185, p. 17
Francie doll, 1966, #1130,
Clear Out!, 1967, #1281, p. 17
Twist 'N Turn Barbie, 1967, #1160, p. 17
Color Magic Barbie, 1967, #1150, p. 17

pp. 18–19
Twigster, 1968, #1727, p. 18
Intrigue, 1968, #1470, p. 18
Dancing Stripes, 1968, #1843, p. 18
Scene Stealers, 1968, #1845, p. 18
Jump into Lace, 1968, #1823, p. 18
Sparkle Squares, 1969, #1814, p. 18
Talking PJ, 1970, #1113, p. 18
Fancy Dancy, 1969, #1858, p. 18
Swirly Cue, 1968, #1822, p. 18
Pretty Power, 1969, #1863, p. 19
Talking Barbie, 1970, #1115, p. 19
Walking Jamie, 1970, #1132, p. 19
Talking Christie, 1970, #1126, p. 19
Talking Brad, 1970, #1114, p. 19
Bendable Leg Ken, 1970, #1124, p. 19
Twist 'N Turn Julia, 1969, #1127, p. 19
Living Barbie, 1970, #1116, p. 19
Living Skipper, 1970, #1117, p. 19
Francie with Growin' Pretty Hair, 1970, #1129, p. 19
Great Coat, 1970, #1459, p. 19

pp. 20–21
Barbie with Growin' Pretty Hair, 1971, #1144, p. 20
Francie in Wild Bunch, 1970, #1766, p. 20
Talking Barbie, 1971, #1115, p. 20
Live Action Barbie on Stage, 1971, #1152, p. 20
Live Action Ken, 1971, #1159, p. 20
Twist 'N Turn Barbie, 1971, #1160, p. 20
Country Camper Vehicle, 1972, #4994, p. 20
The Suede Scene, 1972, #1439, p. 20
Busy Barbie, 1972, #3311, p.20
Malibu Barbie, 1971, #1067, p. 21
Malibu Ken, 1971, #1088, p. 21
Walk Lively Barbie, 1972, #1182, p. 21
Walk Lively Steffie, 1972, #1183, p. 21
Quick Curl Barbie, 1973, #4220, p. 21
Mod Hair Ken, 1973, #4224, p. 21
Baggie Skipper, 1974, #1117, p. 21
Sweet Sixteen, 1974, #7796, p. 21

pp. 22–23
Ten Speeder, 1974, # 7777, p. 22
Growing Up Skipper, 1975, #7259, p. 22
Gold Medal Olympic Skier Ken, 1975, #7261, p. 22
Gold Medal Olympic Barbie, 1975, #7233, p. 22
Hawaiian Barbie, 1976, #7470, p. 22
Deluxe Quick Curl Cara, 1976, #9220, p. 22
Business Suit, 1976, #7246, p. 22
Party time Barbie, 1979, #9925, p. 22
Superstar Christie, 1977, #9950, p. 22
Superstar Ken, 1977, #2211, p. 23
Superstar Barbie, 1977, #9720, p. 23
Now Look Ken, 1976, #9342, p. 23

Supersize Barbie, 1977, #9828, p. 23
Party time Barbie, 1977, #9925, p. 23
Star 'Vette, 1978, #9831, p. 23
Ken wears Casual Suit, 1977, #9167, p. 23
Scott, 1980, #1019, p. 23

pp. 24–25
Black Barbie, 1980, #1293, p. 24
Hispanic Barbie, 1980, #1292, p. 24
Sport and Shave Ken, 1980, #1294, p. 24
Kissing Barbie, 1979, #2597, p. 24
Beauty Secrets Barbie, 1980, #1290, p. 24
My First Barbie, 1981, #1875, p. 24
Happy Birthday Barbie, 1981, #1922, p. 24
Western Barbie, 1981, #1757, p. 24
Dallas, 1981, #3312, p. 24
Golden Dream Christie, 1981, #3249, p. 24
Pink 'N Pretty Christie, 1982, #3555, p. 25
Magic Curl Barbie, 1982, #3856, p. 25
Fashion Jeans Barbie, 1982, #5315
Fashion Jeans Ken, 1982, #5316 , p. 25
Entertainment Center, 1983, #4331, p. 25
Barbie fashion, Evening Rose, 1983, #5548, p. 25
Angel Face Barbie, 1983, #5640, p. 25
Dream Date Barbie, 1983, #5868, p. 25
Dream Date Ken, 1983, #4077, p. 25
Twirly Curls, African-American, 1983, #5723, p. 25
Dream Store Makeup Department, 1983, #4020, p. 25
Garden Party, 1983, #5835, p. 25
Paint the Town Red!, 1983, #5700, p. 25
Sunsational Malibu Barbie, 1983, #1067, p. 25
Sunsational Malibu Skipper, 1983, #1069, p. 25
All Star Ken, 1983, #3553, p. 25

pp. 26–27
My First Barbie, African-American, 1985, #1875, p. 26
Crystal Barbie, 1984, #4598, p. 26
Crystal Ken, 1984, # 4898, p. 26
Peaches 'N Cream Barbie, 1985, #7926, p. 26
Lovin' You Barbie, 1985, #7072, p. 26
Great Shape Barbie, 1985, #7025, p. 26
Day-to-Night Barbie, African American, 1986, #7945, p. 27
Astronaut Barbie, 1986, #2449, p. 27
Rocker Dee-Dee, 1986, #1141, p. 27
Rocker Barbie, 1987, #3055, p. 27
Jewel Secrets Whitney, 1987, #3179, p. 27
Happy Holidays Barbie, 1988, #1703, p. 27
Russian Barbie, Dolls of the World series, 1989, #1916, p. 27
Party Pink Barbie, Customized line, 1989, #7637, p. 27

pp. 28–29
Barbie and the Beat, 1990, #2751, p. 28
Friendship Barbie, 1991, #2080, p. 28
Skipper Party 'N Play Fashion, 1991, A1045, p. 28
My First Ken Fashions:
    "Vested Look", 1991, #4866, p. 28

"Trendy Scarf", 1991, #4865, p. 28
"Muscle Man", 1991, #4864, p. 28
"Cool Sleeping", 1991, #4862, p. 28
Pink Sparkles Magic Table Phone, 1991, #1701, p. 28
Barbie Dinner Date fashion "Blue Dream," 1991, #4938, p. 28
Totally Hair Barbie, 1992, #1117, p. 28
Totally Hair Ken, 1992, #1115, p. 28
Barbie Ferrari, 1992, #3564, p. 28
Stacie doll, 1992, #4240, p. 28
Earring Magic Barbie, 1993, #7014, p. 28
Earring Magic Ken, 1993, #2290, p. 28
Rappin' Rockin' Barbie, 1992, #3248, p. 29
My Size Barbie, 1993, #2517, p. 29
Doctor Barbie, 1994, #11160, p. 29
Camp Fun Barbie 1994, #11074, p. 29
Camp Fun Skipper, 1994, #11076, p. 29
Camp Fun Midge, 1994, #11077, p. 29
Camp Fun Ken, 1994, #11075, p. 29
Camp Fun Teresa, 1994, #11078, p. 29
Gymnast Barbie, 1994, #12127, p. 29
Bedtime Barbie, 1994, #11079, p. 29
Motorcycle Ken, 1994, #12126, p. 29
Kelly doll, 1995, #12489, p. 29
Baywatch Barbie, 1995, #13199, p. 29

pp. 30–31
Olympic Gymnast Barbie, 1996, #15123, p. 30
Flying Hero Barbie, 1996, #10430, p. 30
Share a Smile Becky, 1996, #17247, p. 30
Workin' Out Barbie, 1996, #17317, p. 30
Dentist Barbie, 1997, #17255, p. 30
Teen Skipper, 1997, #17351, p. 30
Beyond Pink Barbie, 1998, #20017, p. 30
Movin' Groovin' Barbie, 1998, #17717, p. 30
Butterfly Art Christie, 1999, #20360, p. 31
Happening Hair, 1999, #22882, p. 31
Shave 'N Style Ken, 1999, #23788, p. 31
Shave 'N Style African-American Ken, 1999, #23937, p. 31
Working Woman™ Barbie, 1999, #20548, p. 31
"Millennium Girl," Fashion Fun Gift set, 1999, #14303, p. 31
Generation Girls: Barbie #19428, Nichelle #20966, Chelsea #20967, (Lara – not shown– #20968), Tori #20969, Ana #20972, 1999, p. 31
Barbie and Baby Sister Krissy, 1999, #22232, p. 31
Happy 40th Anniversary Barbie, 1999, #21384, p. 31

pp. 34–35
Barbie Doll's Dream House, 1961, #816, p. 34–35
Nighty Negligee Set, 1959, #965, p. 34
Sheath Sensation 1961, #986, p. 35
Coffee's On, 1966, #1670, p. 35

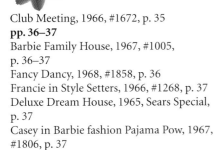

Club Meeting, 1966, #1672, p. 35

pp. 36–37
Barbie Family House, 1967, #1005, p. 36–37
Fancy Dancy, 1968, #1858, p. 36
Francie in Style Setters, 1966, #1268, p. 37
Deluxe Dream House, 1965, Sears Special, p. 37
Casey in Barbie fashion Pajama Pow, 1967, #1806, p. 37

pp. 38–39
Country Living Home, 1973, #8662, p. 38
Twist 'N Turn Busy Barbie doll, 1972, #3311, p. 38
Twist 'N Turn Busy Stefie doll, 1972, #3312, p. 38
Magical Mansion, 1990, #4438, p. 38
Townhouse, 1978, #0711, p. 38
Skipper in "Pink Party Dress,"Best Buy Fashions, 1978, #1078, p. 38
Barbie in "Pink Jumpsuit," 1978, #9966, p. 38
Barbie in "Blue Peignoir Set," Get-Ups 'N Go fashion, 1978, #9743, p. 38
Ken in Now Look Ken doll's "Leisure Suit," 1976, #9342, p. 38
Dream House furnished, 1979, #2587, p. 38
Super Teen Skipper doll, 1979, #2756, p. 38
Pretty Changes Barbie doll, 1979, #2598, p. 38
Kissing Barbie doll, 1979, #2597, p. 38
Superstar Ken doll, 1978, #2211, p. 38
Barbie in "Orange Culottes," Best Buy fashion, 1978, #2222, p. 38
Deluxe Dream House and dog, 1998, #18638, p. 38
Shave 'N Style Ken doll, 1998, #23788, p. 38
Barbie in Purple Prose, Fashion Avenue Boutique, 1998, #20576, p. 39
Skipper in "Fun Wear," Fashion Avenue, 1999, #20623, p. 39
Tommy and Kelly, Jeep Power Wheels, 1998, #18717, p. 39

pp. 40–41
Deluxe Dream House, 1998, #18638, p. 40–41
Barbie Carbriolet car, 1998, #22917 (International only), p. 41
Bowling Party Stacie, 1999, #22013, p. 41
Kelly and Tommy Dolls, Jeep Power Wheel, 1998, #18717, p. 41
Skipper in Fashion Avenue, 1999, #20623, p. 41
Shave 'N Style Ken doll, 1998, #23788, p. 41
Bath Boutique Barbie, 1999, #22357, p. 40

pp. 42–43
Ponytail Barbie in Garden Party, 1962, #931, and What's Cookin', 1964, #1398–4, p. 42
Dream Kitchen-Dinette, 1965, #4095, p. 42
Barbie in On the Avenue, 1965, #1644, p. 42
Barbie in Disc Date, 1965, #1633, p. 42
Ken in Rovin' Reporter, 1965, #1417, p. 42
Barbie Cooking Magic Kitchen, 1998,

#18900, p.42
Jeep Power Wheels Kelly doll, 1998, #18717, p. 42
Barbie in dark brown outfit, Fashion Avenue Boutique, 1999, #23365, p. 42
Skipper in pink outfit, Fashion Avenue Skipper, 1999, #22926, p. 43
Barbie doll's Town & Country Market, 1971, #4984, p. 43
Barbie in Shift into Knit 1969, #1478, p. 43
Country Kitchen, 1975, #7404, p. 43
Free Moving Barbie, 1975, #7270, p. 43
Dream Furniture Collection, 1979:
Refrigerator/Freezer, #2473, p. 43
Stove/Microwave, #2417, p. 43
Barbie in "Plaid," My First Barbie fashion, 1981, #1875, p. 43
Pink Sparkles Collection, 1991:
Cooking Center, #4777, p. 43
Refrigerator/Freezer, # 4776, p. 43
Magic Washer 'N Dryer, #1706, p. 43
Barbie in "Sweater Time," Knit Collection, 1990, #A8031, p. 43

pp. 44–45
Barbie Bed and Bath, 1998, #18605, p. 44–45
Barbie in "Delicate Peignoir," Fashion Avenue Lingerie, 1998, #18093, p. 44
Barbie or Midge Suzy Goose* Queen Size Bed, Chifforobe, and Vanity (*Suzy Goose Furniture manufactured by The Kiddie Brush and Toy Co. of Jonesville, Michigan under license from Mattel Toys)
World of Barbie Beauty Bath, 1976, #9223, p. 45
Barbie in "Floral Jumper," Best Buy Fashion, 1975, #7416, p. 45
Luxury Bathtub, 1980, #1049, p. 45
Bath chest and Commode, 1980, #1045, p. 45
Barbie in Pleasant Dreams, Fashion Favorites, 1980, #1400, p. 45
Dream Bed, 1983 #5641, p.45
Barbie in Lovely 'N Lacy, Fashion Favorites, 1983, #5641, p. 44

pp. 46–47
Barbie in "Lingerie," Barbie Fashion Avenue, Fancy Frills, 1996, #14290, p. 46
"Leopard Look," Fashion Avenue Lingerie, 1999, #22929, p. 46
"Makeup Magic" set, Pretty Treasures Fashion Accessories, #A13758, 1995, p. 46
"Pretty in Pink," Fashion Avenue Lingerie, 1999, #18090, p. 46
Lingerie Sets, Fashion Avenue Lingerie, 1999, #18094, p. 47
Delicate Peignoir and nightdress, Fashion Avenue Lingerie, 1998, #18093, p. 47
"Sea-blue Surprise," Fashion Avenue Lingerie, 1998, #18098, p.47
Floral Petticoat, 1959, #921, p. 47
Nighty Negligee, 1959, #965, p. 47

pp. 50–51
"Daisy Chain," Pretty in Plaid Barbie doll, 1999, #20666, p. 50
City Pretty-green, Fashion Avenue Boutique, 1999, #20577, p. 50

Picnic Set, 1959, #967, p. 50
Fashion Editor, 1965, #1635, p. 50
Quick Curl Cara, 1976, #9220, p. 50
"Purple Prose," Fashion Avenue Boutique, 1999, #20576, p. 51
Green Thumb, Barbara Millicent Roberts fashion ensemble, 1998, #19433, p. 51
"Keep Cool," Fashion Avenue Trend City, 1999, #20646, p. 51
"Easter chic," Easter Style Barbie doll for Specialty Stores, 1998, #17652, p. 51

pp. 52–53
Island Vacation, Fashion Avenue Duo, 2000, #24315, p. 52
"Casual Ken," Fashion Avenue Ken, 1999, #20604, p. 52
Picnic Set, Arco Accessories, 1999, #A68652, p. 52
"Casual Elegance," Fashion Avenue Skipper fashion, 1999, #20627, p. 53
"Cool Kid," Fashion Avenue Kelly Patchwork, 1998, #16697, p. 53
"Toddler Tommy," Big Brother Ken and Baby Brother Tommy dolls, 1997, #17055, p. 53
"Stacie," Bowling Stacie, 1999, #22013, p. 53

pp. 54–55
"Country Cotton," Fashion Avenue, 1999, #A18126, p. 54
"Misty Blue," Sparkle Beach Barbie doll swim suit, 1996, #13132, p. 54
"Denim Suit," Barbie, Floating Cool fashion, 1996, #14374, p. 54
"Banana Belle," Butterfly Art Barbie doll swim suit, 1999, #20359, p. 54
"Dash of Denim," Barbie & Kelly Cuts 'N Color fashion, 1997, #A68600, p. 54
All Decked Out, travel outfit, "Glam 'N Gold" bikini, and accessories, Barbie Millicent Roberts fashion ensemble, 1997, #17568, p. 54–5
Jet Set, Barbie Millicent Roberts Luggage Ensemble, 1997, #17571, p. 54–55
"Everyday Denim," Fashion Avenue, 1998, #18126-1 Asst., p. 55
"Candy Cute," Fashion Avenue,1998, #A68000-96, p. 55
"Lemon Lovely," Fashion Avenue, 1997, #A68580-91, p. 55
"Lime 'N Lilac," Fruity Fun, Grape Fashion, 1999, #A678644-92, p. 55
Hawaiian Barbie, 1975, #7470, p. 55
Malibu Barbie, 1971, #1067, p. 55

pp. 56–57
"Cute Kelly," Cute 'N Cool fashions, 1997, #A68600-91, p. 56
"Florida girl" Barbie, Florida Vacation Barbie doll,1999, #20535, p. 56
"Laid-back Ken," Fashion Avenue Ken, 1999, #23130, p. 56
"Cool and casual" Kira, Butterfly Art Kira doll, 1999, #20362, p. 57
"Surfing Style" Steven, Florida Vacation Steven doll, 1999, #20497, p. 57
"Dazzling Day" Midge, Floatin' 'N Cool Fashion, 1996, #14373, p. 57
"Sunseeker" Christie, Florida Vacation Christie, 1999, #20536, p. 57

Watercraft, Barbie Splash 'N Fun Playset, 1998, #67707-91, p. 56
Windsurfer, Barbie Playpacks, 1999, Wind Surfin' Fun, #67705-91, p. 57

pp. 58–59
"Corduroy Cool," 1999, #24658. p. 58
Fashion Avenue, Boutique series:
"Leather Look," 1999, #20571, p. 58
"Furry Look," 1999, #20579, p. 58
"Stepping Out," 1998, #18139, p. 59
City Slicker, Barbie Millicent Roberts fashion ensemble, 1997, #17570, p. 59
"Nineties Skipper," Fashion Avenue Teen Skipper fashion, 1998,#18381, p. 59
Skipper in Rain or Shine, 1965, #1916, p. 59
Francie in Clam Diggers, 1966, #1258, p. 59
Francie in Snake Charmers, 1970, #1245, p. 59

pp. 60–61
"Red Velvet," Fashion Avenue Matchin' Styles, 1999, #20608, p. 60
"Casual Ken," Fashion Avenue Ken, 1999, #A18099, p. 61
Dalmatian puppy, Pet Lovin' Assortment, Dalmation, 1999, #20849, p. 60

pp. 62–63
"Snow Chic," Snow Chic-So-Chic, Barbie Millicent Roberts Fashion ensemble, 1998, #19772, p. 62
"Misty Mauve," Fashion Avenue Boutique Collection, 1998, #19202, p. 62
"Pink Puff," Fashion Avenue Boutique Collection, 1998, #18135, p. 62
Barbie Coat Collection for Specialty Stores:
"Winter Warmer," 1998, #68650, p. 63
"Diva," 1999, #22156, p. 63
"Furry and Fun," 1999, #22158, p. 63
"Winter Fun," Barbie from Changing Seasons Dress 'N Play Collection for Specialty Stores, 1998, #68652, p. 63
Winter Holiday outfit, 1959, #975, p. 63
Plush Pony outfit, 1969, #1873, p. 63

pp. 64–65
Steven in "Winter Warmer": sweater 1996, #14676, pants and boots, #18099, p. 64
"Snow Sport," Ken Fashion Avenue fashions, 1999, #23131, p. 64
"Blue Frost," Fashion Avenue Coat Collection, Specialty Stores, 1997, #22155, p. 65
Christie in "Ice Maiden," Fashion Avenue Coat Collection, Specialty Stores, 1998, #2216, p. 65

pp. 66–67
Barbie in Dancing Stripes, 1968, #1843, p. 66
Superstar Christie, 1977, #9950, p. 66
"Lovely in Lilac," 1998, #A18155, p. 66
"Pink Flapper," Fashion Avenue Party Collection, 1999, #23118, pp. 66

"Lady in Red," Fashion Avenue Party Collection, 1999, #20589, p. 66

"Gorgeous in Gold," Fashion Avenue Party Collection, 1997,#14365, p. 66

"Day to night," Hollywood Nails Barbie doll, 1999, #17857, p. 67

"Yo-Yo Skipper," Totally Yo-Yo Skipper, 1999, #22228, p. 67

"Pink Shimmer," 1998, #A18379, p. 67

"Short and Sweet," party dress included with Totally Yo-Yo Skipper doll, 1999, #22228, p. 67

"Trendy Twinset," 1999, #20629, p. 67

pp. 68–69

Midge in "Shining Silver," Fashion Fun Gift set for Specialty Stores, 1999, #24148, p. 68

Teresa in "Ice Dancer," Fashion Fun Gift set for Specialty Stores, 1999, #24148, p. 68

Steven in "Sweet Steppin'," Shave 'N Style clothes, 1999, #23937, p. 68

Christie in "Happy Times," Hollywood Nails Christie, 1999, #24557, p. 68

"Starry Night," Hollywood Nails Barbie, 1999, #17857, p. 69

Shave 'N Style Ken, 1999, #23788, p. 69

Kira in "Purple Poise," N.Y. Night, Fashion Avenue Charm, 2000, #24287, p. 69

Totally Yo-Yo Courtney in "Pink Sparkle," 1999, #22230, p.69

Totally Yo-Yo Skipper in "Teen Dream," 1999, #22228, p. 69

pp. 70–71

Christie in "Glamor Girl," Fashion Avenue Boutique fashion, 1999, #20569, p. 70

Barbie in Perfectly Suited, Barbie Millicent Roberts Giftset, 1997, #17567, p. 70

Teresa in "Hippy Chic," Fashion Avenue Trend fashion, #20645, p. 71

"Day Into Night," Barbie Millicent Roberts giftset, 1997, #17567, p. 71

pp. 72–73

London Tour outfit, 1966, #1661, p. 72

Walk Lively Barbie, 1971, #1182, p. 72

"City Jungle," Fashion Trend City, 1999, #20643, p. 72

"Trendy Tie-Dye," Fashion Avenue Boutique, 1999, #23368, p. 72

"City Chic," 1999, #20600, p. 72

"Woven Wonder," 1998, #18137, p. 73

"Winter Warmer," 1996, Barbie Fashion Avenue, #14399, p. 73

"Check-mate," 1998, #18137 p. 73

"Pink Rain," 1999, #18377, p.73

"Purple and Pretty," 1999, #20644, p. 73

The Purse Closet, p. 73

  Day Purses: Fashion Avenue

    Denim Imitation fur, 1996, #14671

      Leather-look, 1996, #14673

    Fun "bubble" purses: Special Collection City Pretty Purple, 1999, #22273, City Pretty Green, 1999, #22296

    Glitzy Night: Fashion Avenue Party Collection Pouch bag, 1997, #15864

      Lilac sparkle, 1997, #15867, Pretty Treasures Collection,

Heart-shaped purse, 1996, #A13759

Silver and purple clasp purses, 1996, #A13759

Envelope clutches: Fashion Avenue Collection Golden sparkle, 1997, #15894

Midnight velvet, 1997, Fashion Avenue Denim, #15866

Pretty in pink, 1998, #23118

pp. 74–75

Kira in "Cool Kira," Country Club Lunch, Fashion Avenue Charm, 2000, #24209, p. 74

Skipper in Barbie doll's "Party in Pink," Fashion Avenue Charm, 2000, #24289, p. 74

Christie in "Pink Charmer," Tea in London, Fashion Avenue Charm, 2000, #24215, p. 75

"Dream Bride," Fashion Avenue Evening Wear, 1999, #20634, p. 75

Midge in "Lady in Lilac," Fashion Avenue Matching Styles, 1999, #20609, p. 75

Kelly in "Flower Girl," Fashion Avenue Matching Styles, 1999, #20609, p.75

pp. 76–77

Box: Forever Love

Wedding Party Gift Set, 1964, #1017, p. 76 included are the following fashions:

  Skipper in Flower Girl, 1964, #1904, p. 76

  Barbie in Bride's Dream, 1963, #947, p. 76

  Ken in Tuxedo, 1961, #0787, p. 76, 77

  Midge in Orange Blossom, 1961, #0987, p. 76, 77

"Spring Bride," Fashion Avenue Bridal, 1998, #17622, p. 76

"Summer Bride," Fashion Avenue Bridal, 1997, #15898, p. 76

"Fall Bride," Fashion Avenue Bridal, 1998, #17625, p. 77

"Winter Bride," Fashion Avenue Bridal, 1998, #17630, p. 77

Ken in "Glitter Groom," Great Date Ken Doll, 1997, #14837, p. 77

pp. 78– 79

Box: Sixties Style

Barbie in Midnight Blue, 1965, #1617, p. 78

Barbie in Evening Gala, 1966, #1660, p. 78

Barbie in Shimmering Magic, 1966, #1664, p. 78

"Night Out," Fashion Avenue Party Collection, 1997, #15866, p. 78

"China Girl," Fashion Avenue Party Collection, 1999, #22924, p. 78

"Dream Date," Fashion Avenue Party Collection, 1999, #20591, p. 78

"Golden Glow," Fashion Avenue Evening Wear, 1999, #20629, p. 79

"Sophisticated Lady," Fashion Avenue Evening Wear, 1996, #14306, p. 79

"Lady in Red," Fashion Avenue Coat Collection for Specialty Stores, 1999, #22157, p. 79

"Golden Touches," Fashion Avenue Accessory Packs, 1999, #20963, p. 79

pp. 80–81

Christie in "Blue Sparkle," 1999, Fashion Avenue Evening Wear, #18120, p. 80

Ken in "Cool Dude," 1999, Fashion Avenue Matchin' Styles for Ken and Tommy dolls, 1999, #18118, p. 80

Teresa in "Golden Girl," Fashion Avenue Evening Wear, 1998, #15894, p. 80

Barbie in "Black Rose," Fashion Avenue Evening Wear, 1999, #19194, p. 81

pp. 84–85

Happy Holidays, Happy Holiday Collection, 1998, #20200, p. 84

Happy Holidays, Happy Holiday Collection, 1989, #3253, p. 84

Pink Splendor, Ultra Limited series, 1996, #16091, p. 84–85

Millennium Princess, 1999, #24154, p. 85

Patriot Barbie, 1997 American Stories Series, #17312, p. 85

1920s Dance 'Till Dawn, Great Fashions of the 20th Century series, 1998, #19631, p. 85

pp. 86–87

The Flamingo Barbie, Birds of Beauty Collection, 1999, #22957, p. 86

Harpist Angel, Angels of Music Collection, 1998, #18894, p. 86

Whispering Wind, Essence of Nature Collection, 1999, #22834, p. 87

Water Lily, Limited Edition, 1997, #17783, p. 87

Autumn Glory, Enchanted Seasons Collection, 1996, #15204, p. 87

Fairy of the Forest, Enchanted World of Fairies, 2000, #25639, p. 87

pp. 88–89

Barbie in Ballerina, 1961, #989, p. 88

Ballerina Barbie, 1976, #9093, p. 88

Swan Lake Barbie, Musical Ballerina Series, 1991, #1648, p. 88

Ballerina Barbie, My First Barbie Series, 1993, #2516, p. 88

Ballerina Dreams, Customized Line, 1998, #28676, p. 88

Solo in the Spotlight, 1961, #982, p. 89

Pink 'N Pretty Barbie, 1983, #3553 , p. 89

Electronic Piano, 1983, #5085, p. 89

Rocker Barbie, 1987, #3055, p. 89

Ice Capades Barbie, 1990, #9847, p. 89

Rappin' Rockin' Barbie, 1992, #3248, p. 89

Beyond Pink Barbie, 1998, #20017, p. 89

pp. 90–91

Registered Nurse, 1961, #991, p. 90

Doctor fashion, 1973, Get-ups 'N Go series, #7700, p. 90

Doctor Barbie, 1988, #3850, p. 90

Dr. Barbie, 1994, #11160, p. 90

Pet Doctor, Caring Careers Gift Set, 1994, #10773, p. 90

Dentist Barbie, 1997, #17255, p. 90

Student Teacher, 1965, #1622, p. 91

Teacher Barbie, 1995, #13194, p. 91

Police Officer Barbie, 1993, #10688, p. 91

Firefighter Barbie, 1994, #13472, p. 91

pp. 92–93

American Airlines Air Stewardess, 1961, #984, p. 92

Pan American Airlines Air Stewardess, 1966, #1678, p. 92

Air Force Barbie, 1990, #3360, p. 92

Navy Barbie, 1991#9693, p. 92

Desert Storm Army Barbie, 1993, #1234, p. 92

Pilot Barbie, 1999, #24017, p. 92

Miss Astronaut, 1965, #1641, p. 92

Astronaut Barbie, 1986, #2449, p. 92

Astronaut Barbie, 1994, #12149, p. 92

Busy Gal, 1960, #981, p. 93

"Office Girl" outfits, Get-Ups 'N Go Fashions, 1978, #9742, p. 93

Day-to-Night Barbie, 1985, African-American #7945, p. 93

Barbie For President, 1991, African-American #3940, blonde, #3722, p. 93

Working Woman™ Barbie, 1999, #20548, p. 93

pp. 94–95

Native American Barbie, American Stories Series, 1997, #17313, p. 94

Dolls of the World Series:

Canadian Barbie, 1988, #4928, p. 94

Northwest Coast Native American Barbie, 2000, #24671, p. 94

Arctic Barbie, 1997, #16495, p.94

Mexican Barbie, 1996, #14449, p. 94

Chilean Barbie, 1998, #18559, p. 95

Peruvian Barbie, 1999, #21506, p. 95

Jamaican Barbie, 1992, #4647, p. 95

Puerto Rican Barbie, 1997, #16754, p. 95

Brazilian Barbie, 1990, #9094, p. 95

pp. 96–97

Irish Barbie, 1995, #12998, p. 96

English Barbie, 1992, #4973, p. 96

Spanish Barbie, 1992, #4963, p. 96

Scottish Barbie, 2nd Edition, 1991, #9845, p. 96

Dutch Barbie, 1994, #15845, p. 96

French Barbie, 1997, #16499, p. 96

Norwegian Barbie, 1996, #14450, p. 97

German Barbie, 1995, #12698, p. 97

Italian Barbie, 1993, # 2256, p. 97

Russian Barbie, 1997, #16495, p. 97

Polish Barbie, 1998, #18560, p. 97

Austrian Barbie, 1999. #21553, p. 97

Czechoslovakian Barbie, 1991, #7330, p.97

pp. 98–99

Moroccan Barbie, 1999, #21507, p.98

Ghanaian Barbie, 1996, #15303, p. 98

Indian Barbie, 1996, #14451, p. 98

Nigerian Barbie, 1990, #7376, p. 98

Kenyan Barbie, 1994, #11181, p. 98

Chinese Barbie, 1994, #11180, p. 99

Thai Barbie, 1998, #18561, p. 99

Korean Barbie. 1988, #4929, p. 99

Japanese Barbie, 1996, #14163, p. 99

Australian Barbie, 1993, #3626, p. 99

Malaysian Barbie, 1991, #7329, p. 99

Polynesian Barbie, 1996, #12700, p. 99

pp. 100–101

Rollerblade Barbie, 1992, #2214, p. 100

Hawaiian Barbie, 1975, #7470, p. 100

Roller Skating Barbie, 1981, #1880, p. 100

Roller Skating Ken, 1981, #1881, p. 100

Ocean Magic Barbie, 1996, #15428, p. 100
Ski Queen outfit, 1963, #948, p. 101
Allan in Ski Champion outfit, 1963, #798, p. 101
Skater's Waltz outfit, 1965, #1629, p. 101
"Winter Fun" Barbie, Changin' Seasons Dress 'N Play Giftset for Specialty Stores, Winter, 1999, #68652, p. 101
Ski Fun Ken, 1992, #7512, p. 101
Ski Fun Barbie, 1992, #7511, p. 101

pp. 102–103
Tennis Anyone?, 1962, #941, p. 102
Hiker Barbie outfit, Get-Ups 'N Go fashion, 1973, #7702, p. 102
Barbie in "Two for Tennis?," Get-Ups 'N Go fashion, 1974, #7842, p. 102
Ken in "Two for Tennis?," Get-Ups 'N Go fashion, 1974, #7837, p. 102
Great Shape Barbie, 1984, #7025, p. 102
Horse Riding Barbie, 1998, #19268, p. 102
Gymnast Barbie, 1994, #12127, p. 102
Olympic Gymnast PJ, 1975, #7263, p. 103
Olympic Skater Barbie, 1975, #7262, p. 103
Olympic Skier Ken, 1975, #7261, p. 103
Paralympic Becky, 2000, #24662, p. 103
Swimming Champion, 2000, #24590, p. 103
Olympic Gymnast Barbie, 1996, #15123, p. 103

pp. 104–105
Benefit Ball Barbie, Classique Collection, 1992, #1521, p. 104
Starlight Dance, Classique Collection, 1996, #15461, p. 105
Givenchy, Limited Edition Designer series, 2000, #24635, p. 105

pp. 106–107
"Celebrity Gala," Bill Blass Barbie doll, Designer Barbie series, 1997, #17040, p. 106
Tangerine Twist, Fashion Savvy Collection, 1998, #17860, p. 106
In the Limelight, Runway Collection, 1997, #17031, p. 107
Evening Illusion, Limited Edition Designer Barbie Series, 1999, #23495, p. 107

pp. 108–109
Gold Barbie, Bob Mackie series, 1990, #5405, p. 108
Neptune Fantasy, Bob Mackie series, 1992, #4248, p. 108
Fantasy Goddess of Asia, Bob Mackie's International Beauty Collection, 1998, #20648, p. 109
Fantasy Goddess of Africa, Bob Mackie's International Beauty Collection, 1999, #23044, p. 109

pp. 110–111
Barbie as Scarlett O'Hara #2, Hollywood Legends Collection, 1995, #12815, p. 110
Barbie as Marilyn Monroe, Hollywood Legends Collection, 1997, #17451, p. 110
Audrey Hepburn in *Breakfast at Tiffany's*, Timeless Treasures Celebrity dolls, 1998, #20355, p. 111

Elizabeth Taylor as Cleopatra, Timeless Treasures Celebrity dolls, 2000, #23595, p. 111

pp. 112–113
Ken and Barbie as Romeo and Juliet, Together Forever Collection, 1998, #19364, p. 112
Nutcracker Barbie, Classic Ballet Series, 1997, #17056, p. 112
Barbie as Dorothy (Judy Garland), Hollywood Legends Collection, 1995, #12701, p. 112
Ken as the Cowardly Lion, Hollywood Legends Collection, 1997, #16573, p. 113
Ken as the Tin Man, Hollywood Legends Collection, 1996, #14902, p. 113
Rosie O'Donnell, Celebrity Friends of Barbie Series, 1999, #22016, p. 113
Barbie and Ken, Star Trek Giftset, 1996, Pop Culture Series, #15006, p. 113

pp. 114–115
Barbie in Suburban Shopper, 1959, #969, p. 114
Ken and his Friends and Family
Ken, 1961, #750, p. 114
Allan, 1964, #1000, p. 114
Brad, 1970, #1142, p. 114
Curtis, 1975, #7282, p. 114
Todd, 1983, #4253, p. 114
Derek, 1986, #2428, p. 114
Steven, 1988, #4093, p. 114
Tommy, brother, 1997, #17055, p. 114
Friends of Barbie
Midge, Best Friend, 1963, #860, p. 115
Christie, 1968, #1162, p. 115
Stacey, 1968, #1165, p. 115
PJ, 1969, #1113, p. 115
Jamie, 1970, #1132, p. 115
Steffie, 1972, #1183, p. 115
Kelley, 1973, #4221, p. 115
Cara, 1975, #7283, p. 115
Tracy, 1983, #4103, p. 115
Diva, 1986, #2427, p. 115
Dee Dee, 1986, #1141, p. 115
Dana, 1986, #1196, p. 115
Whitney, 1987, #3179, p. 115
Miko, 1987, #2056, p. 115
Bopsy, 1988, #4967, p. 115
Belinda, 1988, #4976, p. 115
Becky, 1988, #4977, p. 115
Teresa, 1988, #5503, p. 115
Kayla, 1989, #3512, p. 115
Devon, 1989, #3513, p. 115
Nikki, 1989, #1132, p. 115
Kira, 1990, #4120, #4120, p. 115
Nia, 1990, #9933, p. 115
Tara Lynn, 1993, #10295, p. 115
Shani, 1994, #10958, p. 115
Becky, 1997, #17247, p. 115
Ana, 1999, #20972, p. 115
Chelsie, 1999, #20967, p. 115
Lara, 1999, #20968, p. 115
Michelle, 1999, #20966, p. 115
Tori, 1999, #20969, p. 115
Barbie Doll's Family and their Friends
Skipper, sister, 1964, #950, p. 114
Friends of Skipper
Ricky, 1965, #1090, p. 114
Skooter, 1965, #1040, p. 114
Fluff, 1971, #1143, p. 114

Tiff, 1972, #1199, p. 114
Ginger, 1976 #9222, p. 114
Scott, 1980, #1019, p. 114
Courtney, 1989, #1952, p. 114
Kevin, 1990, #9325, p. 114
Nikki, 1997, #17353, p. 114
Tutti, sister, 1966, #3550, p. 115
Todd, brother, 1966, #3556, p. 115
Francie, cousin, 1966, #1130, p. 115
Jazzie, cousin, 1989, #3635, p. 115
Stacie, sister, 1992, #4240, p. 115
Kelly, sister, 1995, #12489, p. 115
Krissy, baby sister, 1999, #22232, p. 115
Friends of Tutti
Chris, 1967, #3570, p. 115
Friends of Francie
Casey, 1967, #1180, p. 115
Friends of Jazzie
Stacie, 1989, #3636, p. 115
Chelsie, 1989, #3698, p. 115
Dude, 1989, #3637, p. 115
Friends of Stacie
Whitney, 1994, #11476, p. 115
Janet, 1994, #11477, p 115
Friends of Kelly
Chelsie, 1996, #14852, p. 115
Becky, 1996, #14853, p. 115
Melody, 1996, #14854, p. 115
Marissa, 1998, #16002, p. 115
Jenny, 1998, #16467, p. 115
Deidre, 1998, #16466, p. 115
Keeya, 1998, #18917, p. 115
Kayla, 1999, #20855, p. 115
Nia, 1999, #20860, p. 115
Tamika, 1999, #18916, p. 115
Maria, 1999, #20957, p. 115

pp. 116–117
Ken with flocked hair, 1961, #750, p. 116
Ken with painted hair, 1962, #750, p. 116
Busy Ken, 1972, #3314, p. 116
Sunsational Malibu Ken, 1981, #3849, p. 116
Hawaiian Fun Ken, 1991, #5941, p. 116
Shave 'N Style Ken, 1999, #23788, p. 116
Curtis, 1974, #7282, p. 116
Alan, 1991, #9607, p. 116
Skipper, 1964, #950, p. 117
Quick Curl Skipper, 1973, #4223, p. 117
Ricky, 1965, #1090, p. 117
Scott, 1980, #1019, p. 117
Babysitter Skipper, 1991, #9433, p. 117
Kevin, 1990, #9325, p. 117
Cool Sitter Skipper, 1998, #20334, p. 117
Stacie, 1999, #22013, p. 117
Francie, 1966, #1130, p. 117
Skooter, 1965, #1040, p. 117
Tutti, 1966, #3550, p. 117
Hawaiian Fun Jazzie, 1990, #9294, p. 117
Todd, 1991, #9852, p. 117
Krissy, 1999, #22232, p. 117
Kelly and Tommy, Jeep Power Wheels, 1998, #18717, p 117

pp. 118–119
Straight Leg Midge, 1963, #1080, p. 118
Twist 'N Turn Stacey, Night Lightening Sears Giftset, 1969, #1591, p. 118
Talking PJ, 1970, #1113, p. 118
Talking Christie, 1968, #1126, p. 118
Malibu Skipper #1069, Christie #7745, Barbie #1067, Ken #1088, 1978, p. 118

Teresa, Customized Puzzle doll, 1998, #3270, p. 118
Walking Jamie, Sears Giftset, 1970, #1132, p. 118
Wedding Day Midge, 1991, #9606, p. 118
Walk Lively Steffie, 1972, 1183, p. 118
Quick Curl Kelley, 1973, #422l, p. 118
Tracy Bride, 1983, #4103, p. 119
Todd Groom, 1983, #4253, p. 119
All American Kira, 1991, #9427
All-American Christie, #9425, Ken #9424, Barbie #9423, 1991, p. 119
Doctor Shani, 1994, #11814, p. 119
Share a Smile Becky, 1997, #17247, p. 119
Box: Barbie Pets
Dog 'N duds, 1964, #1613, p. 119
Beauty and puppies, 1982, #5019, p. 119
Blinking Beauty horse, 1988, #5087, p. 119
All-American horse, 1991, #2575, p. 119
Tag Along Tiffy, 1993, #3375, p. 119
Sachi, 1992, #5468, p. 119
Puppy Ruff, 1995, #11069, p. 119.

pp.120–121
Barbie #1, 1959, #850, p. 120
Barbie #5, 1961, #850, p. 120
Miss Barbie, 1964, #1060, p. 120
Twist 'N Turn Barbie, 1967, #1160, p. 121
Malibu Barbie, 1972, #1067, p. 121
Superstar Barbie, 1977, #9720, p. 121
Angel Face Barbie, 1983, #5640, p. 121
Bath Boutique Barbie, 1999, #22357, p. 121
"Barbie Today," Jewel Girl Barbie, 2000, #28066, p. 121

pp. 122–123
Barbie doll case, 1961, p. 122
Barbie doll Hatbox, 1961, p. 122
Barbie doll case, 1963, #390, p. 122
Ken doll case, 1962, p. 122
Barbie Fashion Pack, 1962, #A905, p. 122
Ken Fashion Pack, 1962, #A757, p. 122
Ensemble Pack for Modern Art, 1965, #1625, p. 122
Barbie and Midge Duet-Doll case and Wardrobe Carrier, 1963, #300, p. 122
Ensemble Pack for Student Teacher, 1965, #1622, p. 122
Trade doll box, 1959, #850, p. 122
Barbie doll box, 1959, #850, p. 122
Ken doll box, 1961, #750, p. 123
Midge doll box, 1963, #860, p. 123
Allan doll box, 1964, #1000, p. 123
Skipper doll box, 1965, #1030, p. 123
Ricky doll box, 1965, #1090, p. 123
Skooter doll box, 1966, #1120, p. 123
Francie doll box, 1971, #1074, p. 123
Teen Fashion Pack for Barbie Dressmakers, 1964, #1831, p. 123
Junior Fashion Pack for Skipper, 1967, #A1375, p. 123
Francie doll case, 1966, #3002, p. 123
The World of Barbie doll case, 1969, #1002, p. 123
Barbie Traveling Carrying case, 1965, #3505, p. 123
Barbie and Francie Duet-doll case, 1966, #3003, p. 123
Tutti doll case, 1965, #3561, p. 123

INDEX

A

anniversary dolls
    25th 26
    40th 31

B

baggie dolls 21
Barbie
    Angel Face 120
    Bath Boutique 121
    changing face of 120–121
    first 9, 12, 120
    Jewel Girl Barbie 121
    Malibu 21, 55, 121
    Miss Barbie 15, 120
    My First 24, 26
    My Size 29
Barbie and the Rockers 27, 89
Baywatch™ 29
bathrooms 40, 45
Beat, the 28
bedrooms 37, 44, 45
Beyond Pink 89
Bild Lilli doll 9
Blass, Bill 106
Breakfast at Tiffany's 111

C

Campbell, Naomi 31
careers 88–93
    air stewardess 92
    armed forces 92
    astronaut 92
    ballerina 88
    business woman 93
    dentist 30, 90
    doctor 29, 90
    fashion designer 12, 93
    firefighter 91
    nurse 90
    pet doctor 90
    performer 89
    pilot 92
    police officer 91
    presidential candidate 93
    registered nurse 13
    teacher 91
carrying cases 122–123
cars

Austin Healey 13
    Cabriolet 41
    Ferrari 28
    Star 'Vette 23
catwalk dolls 104–107
Charlie's Angels 23
Chatty Cathy 9
clothes selections
    bridal outfits 74–77
    city 72–73
    dancing 66–69
    disco 66–67
    garden 51
    glamorous 78–81
    out on the town 70–71
    party 78–81
    vacation 54–57
    see also fashions
collectibles 84–85
Collections
    Angels of Music 86
    Birds of Beauty 86
    Classique 104–107
    Enchanted Seasons 87
    Enchanted World of Fairies 87
    Essence of Nature 87
    Famous Artists 87
    Fashion Savvy 106
    Hollywood Legends 110
    International Beauty 109
    Runway 107
    Together Forever 112
couturier collections 104–107

D

Diana, Princess 27
dolls, a history 8–9
    baby 8, 9
    paper 8
    teenage 9
    Victorian 8
Dolls of the World, The, series 27, 95–99
    Africa, Asia, and Australasia 98–99
    Europe 96–7
    North and Central America 94
    South America and the Caribbean Islands 95

E, F

exchange deal 17

family of Barbie 114–117
    Francie (cousin) 17, 20, 114, 117
    Jazzie (cousin) 114, 117
    Kelly (sister) 53, 75, 114, 117
    Krissy (sister) 31, 114, 117
    Skipper (sister) 15, 22, 30, 53, 59, 67, 69, 76, 114, 117
    Stacie (sister) 28, 53, 114, 117
    Todd (brother) 114, 117
    Tutti (sister) 114, 117
fantasy dolls 86–97, 108–109
fashions
    by eras:
    Eighties 24–27
    Nineties 28–31
    Seventies 20–23
        Panels: 50, 55, 66, 72
    Sixties 12–19
        Panels: 47, 50, 59, 63, 66, 72, 78
    by seasons:
    fall 58–61
    spring 50–53
    summer 54–57
    winter 62–65
Fonda, Jane 26
friends of Barbie 31, 114–119
    Ana 31, 115
    Becky 30, 115, 119
    Belinda 115
    Bopsy 115
    Cara 22, 115
    Casey 17, 114
    Chelsie 31, 115
    Christie 19, 115, 118
    Courtney 69, 115
    Dana 115
    Dee Dee 27, 115
    Devon 115
    Diva 115
    Jamie 19, 115, 118
    Julia 19
    Kayla 115
    Kelley 115, 118
    Kevin 114, 117
    Kira 69, 115, 119
    Lara 31, 115
    Midge 15, 68, 76, 77, 115, 118
    Miko 115
    Nia 115
    Nichelle 31, 115
    Nikki 115

PJ 18, 103, 115, 118
    Ricky 16, 114, 117
    Scott 23, 114, 117
    Shani 115, 119
    Skooter 16, 114, 117
    Stacey 115, 118
    Steffie 21, 115, 119
    Tara Lynn 115
    Teresa 68, 115, 118
    Tori 31, 115
    Tracy 115
    Twiggy 17, 18
    Whitney 27, 115
friends and family of Ken
    Allan (Alan) 15, 115, 116
    Brad 19, 115
    Curtis 115, 116
    Derek 115
    Steven 57, 68, 115, 116
    Todd 115
    Tommy (brother) 53, 115
furniture 35

G, H

Gentlemen Prefer Blondes 110
Givenchy 105
Gone With the Wind 110
Hammer, MC 29
Handler, Ruth 9
Hepburn, Audrey 111
homes
    Deluxe Dream House 37, 40–41
    Dream House 34–35, 38
    Family House 36
    Magical Mansion 38
    Town House 38
    Houston, Whitney 27

K

Ken 13, 19–31, 115, 116
    see also friends and family of Ken
kitchens 40, 42–43

L

Lars, Bryon 107
limited edition dolls 84
lingerie 46–47

M

Mackie, Bob 108–109
Madonna 27
Miller, Nolan 107

Miss Barbie 15, 120
Monet 87
Monroe, Marilyn 110

N, O

Nightwear 46–47
O'Donnell, Rosie 113
O'Hara, Scarlett 110

P

packaging 122–123
Parton, Dolly 24
Patridge Family, the 21
Perkins, Kitty Black 106
pets
    dogs 60, 61, 119
    horses 24, 119
Pitt, Brad 31
purses 73

S

Saturday Night Fever 23
Schiffer, Claudia 31
series
    Adventures in Space 27
    Classic Ballet 112
    Great Fashions of the 20th Century 85
    Happy Holiday 84
    Timeless Treasures 111
    Ultra Limited 84
    see also Collections, Dolls of the World, The,
    Spencer, Carol 104
Spice Girls, the 30
sports
    keeping fit 102
    Olympic 103
    summer 100
    winter 101
stage, screen, and television 110–113
Star Trek 113

T

Taylor, Elizabeth 111
Travolta, John 23
Turner, Tina 24

W, Y

Wizard of Oz, The 112
Young, Cynthia 105

ACKNOWLEDGMENTS

Dorling Kindersley would like to thank the following for their kind permission to reproduce their photographs:

a=above, c=center, b=below, l=left, r=right, t=top

Aquarius Library: 24cr. Barnaby's Picture Library: 17cr, 18br. Geoff Brightling 99c, 94ar (Pitt Rivers Museum). Johnathan Buckley 99al. Corbis UK Ltd: 31br. Andy Crawford ar. Mary Evans Picture Library: Johyn Maclellan 8b. Neil Fletcher 97br. Roger Phillips 99br. Ronald Grant Archive: 24tr. Robert Harding Picture Library: Ellen Rodney 97tr. Hulton Getty: 8cr, 9tl, 14tr, 17c, 17bc, 19c. Liz McAulay 96bc. Moviestore Collection: 24ca. Pictorial Press Ltd: 94cl, 99cl. Pitt Rivers Museum 98al. Rex Features: 21tl, 23tc. Tim Ridley 94br. Vin Mag Archive: 22br. Barnabas and Anabel Kindersley

Dorling Kindersley would like to thank the following for their kind permission to use their names and marks:

Bill Blass doll: With thanks to Bill Blass Ltd.
Water lily doll: With permission of the Design & Artist Copyright Society
Givenchy doll: With the permission of Givenchy in New York, USA.

Marilyn Monroe doll: Gentlemen Prefer Blondes ™ & © 1953, 2000 Twentieth Century Fox Film Corporation. All rights reserved. Estate of Marilyn Monroe licensed by CMG Worldwide Inc.
Audrey Hepburn doll in Breakfast at Tiffany's: Courtesy of Paramount Pictures. Breakfast at Tiffany's © 2000 by Paramount Pictures. All rights reserved. With kind permission of the Audrey Hepburn Estate. With thanks to Tiffany & Company. "Tiffany" is a registered trademark of Tiffany & Company. The Mark is used with permission of the trademark owner.
Star Trek doll: Courtesy of Paramount Pictures. Star Trek © 2000 by Paramount Pictures. All rights reserved.
The Wizard of Oz and all related characters and elements are trademarks of Turner Entertainment Co. © 2000. Gone With the Wind: Its characters and elements are trademarks of Turner Entertainment Co. & The Stephens Mitchell Trusts. © 2000 Turner Entertainment Co. These dolls were created by Warner Bros. consumer Products and Mattel. For Warner Bros: Kelly Gilmore, Steve Fogelson, Michael Sanchez, Kimberly La Follette.
Bob Mackie dolls: With thanks to Bob Mackie.
Bryon Lars doll: With thanks to Bryon Lars.

Elizabeth Taylor doll: Permission granted by Berkowitz and Associates on behalf of Elizabeth Taylor. Warren Cowan & Associates. Cleopatra ™ & © 1963, 2000 Twentieth Century Fox Film Corporation. All rights reserved. Elizabeth Taylor © 1999 Interplanet Productions Limited, used under license.
Olympic Barbie With thanks to the United States Olympic Committee.
Nolan Miller doll: With thanks to Nolan Miller.
Baywatch™ Barbie: The Licensing Group Ltd.
Ferrari car: courtesy of Ferrari
Working Woman Barbie™: Working Woman is a registered trademark of MacDonald Communications Corporation.
Rosie O'Donnell doll: Used under license to Mattel, Inc from The For All Kids Foundation, Inc.
Corvette car: Vette, Corvette Emblems and Body Designs are General Motors Trademarks used under license to Mattel, Inc.
Dorling Kindersley would like to thank the following people for their assistance on the project:
Tanya Tween, Gary Hyde, Goldy Broad, Rebecca Knowles, Fiona Munro, Cynthia O'Neill. Lynn Bresler for the index.